# COMPREHENSIVE EDUCATION IN ACTION

Edited by
**T. G. Monks**

National Foundation
for Educational
Research in
England and Wales

*Published by the National Foundation for Educational Research
in England and Wales*

*The Mere, Upton Park, Slough, Bucks
and at 79 Wimpole Street, London, W1M 8EA*

*First Published 1970*

© *National Foundation for Educational Research
in England and Wales*

SBN   901225   51   7

Cover design by
PETER GAULD FSIA

*Printed in Great Britain by*
KING, THORNE & STACE LTD., SCHOOL ROAD, HOVE, SUSSEX

# Preface

IN THE early planning of this stage of the NFER's Comprehensive Education project, each research worker was responsible for a certain area of work, the collection of the data, their analysis and presentation. Staff changes have meant, however, that it has not been possible to adhere to this plan in several of the special studies. Nor, indeed, would one wish it to be so, for the research officers have worked as a team, contributing to both their own field of interest and those of others. Although the names of the research worker or workers mainly responsible for each chapter are indicated where appropriate, we would like here to give a fuller picture of the contribution of each.

Mr. A. W. Bates and Miss M. I. Reid were responsible for the sections on school administration and pupils' extra-curricular activities respectively. The section on the curriculum and pupil welfare is by Mr. T. S. Robertson. He received a great deal of help from Mrs. P. Evison and Miss J. Moon (a technical officer who worked with this project for one year) in classifying and analysing the diverse data received from the schools. He also drew upon data collected for the attainment survey. The sections on contacts with the community and on the mixing and friendship patterns of pupils were initiated by Dr. T. Kawwa; he devised the methods, undertook the field work and initial analysis: this work was continued by Mr. Robertson and it is he who wrote the text of this chapter. The early planning of the attainment survey was directed by Mr. Robertson but it is otherwise the work of Mrs. Evison, who administered the tests, analysed the results and wrote the text.

Mr. T. G. Monks, the leader of this team for nearly four years, was unfortunately unable to see this report through to its completion. As his successor I have helped in the general production and editing of this publication. Chapter One is based on earlier drafts done by Mr. Monks and in the final chapter I have drawn on the work of all members of the team.

J. M. Ross

# Acknowledgements

IN AN exercise of this size and kind, the number of people to whom one is indebted is immense, and omission from this list must not be taken as ingratitude.

Our thanks must first of all go to the heads of the schools involved in the work and those members of staff who gave time to our enquiries. Without their co-operation the study would not have been possible. A number of schools also co-operated with us at the 'trying-out' stage of the questionnaires and interview schedules, and to the heads and members of staff of these schools we also extend our thanks.

The Consultative Committee for Research into Comprehensive Education has given sympathetic hearing and ready support throughout the work and our thanks are especially due to those members who so readily gave advice 'extra-murally' to my research officers and myself.

We are grateful too, for the ready co-operation of the Department of Education and Science, Cardiff, in allowing us to use the Welsh Reading Test devised and produced by H.M. Inspectorate and translating some of our own tests into Welsh. In this same area a special word of thanks should go to Mr. I. L. James, Headmaster (at the time of the survey) of one of the Welsh schools, who so readily volunteered to translate other tests into Welsh.

Within the Foundation one at all times enjoys a high level of help and co-operation from one's colleagues, and mention of names could be invidious. We must, however, acknowledge the critical and constructive advice of the Director and Deputy Director, Dr. S. Wiseman and Dr. D. A. Pidgeon, especially in the final drafting of this report. It is important, also, to record our appreciation of the vital assistance given us by the Statistics Department.

Many people have helped with the secretarial work of this project over the years, and to mention them all by name would be impossible. I would however, like to record a special 'thank you' to Miss Vivien Clements, Miss Carol Brennan and Miss Tracy Gradziel, each of whom made a major contribution to the running of this study, and Mrs. Stephanie Box and Mrs. June Klenczon who are currently with the project and typed the final drafts and typescript of this publication.

## Acknowledgements

Finally, a very special mention should be made of Miss Janet Moon who, although her name does not appear as one of the authors, gave splendid and unstinting background help to us all.

T. G. MONKS

# Consultative Committee on Research into Comprehensive Education

## Consultative Committee

### Non-Departmental Representatives Attending in Official Capacity

Dr. S. Wiseman
Director,
National Foundation for
  Educational Research,
The Mere, Upton Park,
Slough.

Dr. J. M. Ross
National Foundation for
  Educational Research,
The Mere, Upton Park,
Slough.

Dr. D. A. Pidgeon,
Deputy Director,
National Foundation for
  Educational Research,
The Mere, Upton Park,
Slough.

R. Sumner, Esq.
Department of Education,
The University,
Manchester 13.

### Department of Education and Science

Miss W. P. Harte
(Schools Branch).

Mr. W. R. Elliott
(HMI).

Mr. B. E. Thomas
(HMI).

Mr. J. A. Richards
(Schools Branch).

Prof. W. Taylor
Bristol University,
Senate House,
Bristol 2.

Mr. W. L. Lloyd
(HMI).

Mr. S. E. Gunn
(HMI).

### Secretariat

Mr. N. W. Stuart
(Secretary),
DES Schools Branch.

Mr. M. Lyons
DES Schools Branch.

Mr. G. Davies
DES Schools Branch.

10

# Contents

*page*

PREFACE     5

ACKNOWLEDGEMENTS     7

MEMBERS OF THE CONSULTATIVE COMMITTEE     9

LIST OF TABLES     13

LIST OF DIAGRAMS     15

1. A Description of the Study     17
   *What is a comprehensive school?; the sample of schools; the collection of information.*

2. The Administration of Comprehensive Schools. By     25
   A. W. BATES
   *Staffing; additional allowances; the distribution of allowances within the school; internal organization; the duties of senior staff; the 'classroom' teacher; the role of pupils in school administration; summary.*

3. The School Curriculum and Pupil Welfare. By T. S.     60
   ROBERTSON
   *Timetabling devices; the first to third years; the fourth and fifth years; the sixth form; the deployment of staff in comprehensive schools; libraries in comprehensive schools; summary.*

4. Attainment Survey. By P. EVISON     100
   *Tests used; test score results; 'X' and 'Z' pupils; test score results for schools of various types; test score results in Welsh schools; summary.*

# Contents

page

5. Mixing and Friendship Choices. By T. KAWWA and
T. S. ROBERTSON                                                                118

*The popularity of different groups; in- and out-group
preferences; between-school difference of inward-
directed choices; summary.*

6. Voluntary Extra-Curricular Activities. By M. I. REID     128

*The scope of the study; school policy towards extra-
curricular activity; pupil participation in extra-curricular
activities; environmental factors and participation in
extra-curricular activities; summary.*

7. Contacts Between the School and the Community. By
T. KAWWA and T. S. ROBERTSON                               169

*School functions and activities; parent-teacher associa-
tions; relationships with former pupils; school magazines
and other publications; relationships with other schools
and educational organizations; visits to factories, farms
and commercial firms; voluntary social work by staff; non-
teaching staff; school courses of study on community
relationship; community consciousness in the schools.*

8. A Look Back and Forward                                 175

APPENDIX A   Tables not Included in the Text               180

APPENDIX B   Index Scores for Determining the Strength of
Various Systems of Internal School Organization            194

*Pupil welfare activities; allowances; time; buildings;
'strong' and 'weak' systems; conclusions; scale for
determining strengths of systems.*

APPENDIX C   Definitions                                   199

LIST OF REFERENCES                                         200

INDEX                                                      202

# List of Tables

*page*

| | | |
|---|---|---|
| 1.1 | Sample of schools related to year of becoming fully developed, size, and sex of pupils | 21 |
| 2.1 | The allocation of special allowances | 31 |
| 2.2 | The functional systems of organization for pupil welfare | 38 |
| 2.3 | Size of school and hours worked by classroom teachers | 51 |
| 2.4 | Number of minutes in the timetable cycle | 53 |
| 3.1 | Curriculum in the first year in one school (School 253) | 72 |
| 3.2 | Mean scores of pupils doing various vocational courses in the fourth year (School 127) | 76 |
| 3.3 | Mean scores of pupils transferring to senior high schools two years later (School 253) | 78 |
| 3.4 | Fourth-year curriculum (two-stream. School 371) | 78 |
| 3.5 | Fourth-year curriculum (large urban. School 273) | 79 |
| 3.6 | Subject options for fourth-years in a large urban school (School 273) | 80 |
| 3.7 | One day in the fourth-form timetable of a comprehensive school (School 273) | 82 |
| 3.8 | Average numbers of sixth-formers in 18 schools | 87 |
| 3.9 | Pupils in four contrasting sixth forms | 88 |
| 3.10 | Courses taken by first-year sixth pupils in four contrasting sixth forms | 88 |
| 3.11 | The 'A' level subjects available in four contrasting sixth forms | 89 |
| 3.12 | The option-block system of sixth-form subjects in comprehensive school 273 | 92 |
| 3.13 | Time spent by teachers with sixth forms and more able pupils in school 136 (percentages) | 95 |
| 3.14 | Average expenditure on school libraries | 97 |
| 4.1 | First-year NF68 mean and standard deviation scores | 102 |
| 4.2 | Percentile distributions for first-year NF68 scores | 103 |
| 4.3 | Fourth-year NF68 mean and standard deviation scores | 104 |
| 4.4 | Percentile distributions for fourth-year NF68 scores | 104 |
| 4.5 | Mean scores for the CP66 aptitude test | 105 |

## List of Tables

|      |                                                                                    | page |
|------|------------------------------------------------------------------------------------|------|
| 4.6  | CP66 population mean and standard deviation scores                                  | 105  |
| 4.7  | Total test scores and age range of pupils                                          | 108  |
| 4.8  | Total test scores and competition with grammar schools                             | 109  |
| 4.9  | Total test scores and urban/rural location                                         | 110  |
| 4.10 | Total test scores and geographical region                                          | 111  |
| 4.11 | Total test scores and school origin                                                | 111  |
| 4.12 | Total test scores and size of school                                               | 112  |
| 4.13 | First-year NF68 scores                                                             | 113  |
| 4.14 | Fourth-year NF68 scores                                                            | 114  |
| 4.15 | First-year sixth CP66 scores                                                       | 114  |
| 4.16 | Welsh and English reading test scores                                              | 115  |
| 4.17 | Ranking of NF68 test scores for Welsh schools                                      | 116  |
| 5.1  | Relative popularity of different groups (eight schools)                            | 120  |
| 5.2  | Distribution of choices among ability groups (School 314)                          | 121  |
| 5.3  | Distribution of choices among behaviour groups (School 314)                        | 122  |
| 5.4  | 'In-group' preference and ability                                                  | 123  |
| 5.5  | 'In-group' preference and social class                                            | 123  |
| 5.6  | 'In-group' preference and behaviour                                               | 124  |
| 5.7  | Rank order of index of preference                                                  | 125  |
| 5.8  | Overall indices of preference in separate schools                                  | 126  |
| 6.1  | Non-participation in activities                                                    | 141  |
| 6.2  | High participation in activities                                                   | 141  |
| 6.3  | Year-group and participation (pupils at mixed all-through schools only)            | 145  |
| 6.4  | Ability and Participation                                                          | 148  |
| 6.5  | The estimated ability of sixth-form pupils                                         | 153  |
| 6.6  | Participation of sixth-formers compared with pupils in years 1-5                   | 154  |
| 6.7  | Social class and participation—4 rural schools                                     | 156  |
| 6.8  | Social class and participation—4 urban schools                                     | 157  |
| 6.9  | Social class, ability and participation—analysis of variance (significance levels) | 158  |
| 6.10 | Homework time and participation—mean number of activities                          | 161  |
| 6.11 | Hours per week spent on activities by participant staff according to sex and marital status | 164  |

# List of Diagrams

*page*

2.1   Allowances for posts of responsibility   30

2.2   Size of school and proportion of allowances given to academic subjects or administrative and pupil welfare responsibilities   33

2.3   Total of estimates (in hours) for 'classroom' teachers' activities   50

3.1   The distribution of ability in intake (School 209)   64

3.2   The distribution of ability in four sets of first-year pupils (School 029)   65

3.3   The distribution of ability of first-year pupils in seven streams (School 253)   67

3.4   The distribution of ability of first-year pupils in three broad ability bands (School 314)   68

3.5   Percentages of first-year pupils with fathers in different occupations (School 063)   69

3.6   The distribution of ability of fourth-year pupils in three streams (School 192)   75

3.7   Percentages of fourth-year pupils with fathers in different occupations (School 028)   77

6.1   Year-group and participation: percentage of non-participants   143

6.2   Year-group and participation: percentage of high-participants   144

6.3   Sex, year-group and participation (12 mixed all-through schools)   146

6.4   Ability and participation: percentage of non-participants   151

6.5   Ability and participation: percentage of high-participants   152

6.6   Homework time and participation (12 mixed all-through schools)   162

15

# CHAPTER ONE

# A Description of the Study

*C*OMPREHENSIVE *Education in England and Wales. A Survey of Schools and their Organization* by T. G. Monks (1968) was the first report of the Foundation's comprehensive education project; it gave a description of the overall structure of comprehensive education as it existed at that time, when 222 of the 331 schools studied were fully developed comprehensive schools with a complete age-range of pupils. The information for the first part of the study came from the headmasters and headmistresses and members of their staffs. Topics covered in this first large-scale survey included the origin of the schools and their type as defined by the Department of Education and Science; their internal organization and administration; the estimated ability of the pupils and their social class; transfer between streams; sixth-form size; extra-curricular activities and the qualifications and employment of the staff. The plans for this research date from 1965, the year in which local authorities were requested by the Secretary of State to 'prepare and submit to him plans for the reorganization of secondary education in their areas on comprehensive lines' (Circular 10/65).

Since then five years have passed and of the 163 authorities in England and Wales, 130 have had their schemes approved for the whole or part of their areas. Those of a further 11 are now being considered and five have yet to submit their plans. On the other hand, nine have had their schemes rejected and eight have declined to submit any non-selective proposals.

Such major re-planning of secondary education is bound to present enormous problems of administration, organization and finance; also the overall lack of knowledge and experience and the general heat of the arguments for and against comprehensive schools have tended to obscure rational and clear thinking. The purpose of the first and also of this present report is to produce facts and figures in this area, for there exists relatively little objective and impartial evidence covering a considerable number of schools.

This, then, is the survey of an evolving system of secondary

17

education, a system growing up in what is often a competitive situation. From the facts and figures which emerge it will be seen how the pioneers have approached their tasks, and some of their problems will be identified.

The project was announced by the Secretary of State for Education and Science in September, 1965; it got under way some six months later under the guidance of a Consultative Committee[1] chaired by Mr. H. F. Rossetti. The investigation was seen as an important and integral part of the change to a fully comprehensive system—the planners, organizers and those responsible for education needed a factual body of information about comprehensive schools and their pupils as well as some evaluation of the extent to which the aims of comprehensive education were being realized in those schools. The study was planned in a series of stages, the first to be descriptive only, providing part of the information mentioned above. The second would complete this picture by surveying certain specialized fields in greater detail. The final stage will be evaluative.

The first survey, as already mentioned, covered 331 schools; the second, reported here, includes 59, and for the final evaluative stage we have been promised the full co-operation of the 12 schools approached. Thus the study which was large-scale and descriptive at its inception has narrowed the focus of its attention. This book summarizes the investigation based on the smaller sample of 59 schools and in the final stage a case study approach will be adopted.

At the time of writing, the final stage (evaluating the extent to which the schools are achieving the aims of comprehensive education and their level of success) is just commencing. This should be regarded as a co-operative effort between the members of a special committee (consisting of two sub-groups, 'the practitioners' and 'the theorists', the Department of Education in the University of Manchester, the Sociology Department in the University of Liverpool and the Foundation. The two groups of the special committee produced an agreed list of the aims of comprehensive education and it has been the task of the other three bodies to devise tests and questionnaires to measure the degree to which the schools are achieving these objectives or goals. The number of schools in this last stage is of necessity limited. This is due both to the complexity and length of the testing programme and to the fact that this stage also serves as a pilot investigation using individual schools to develop instruments that may later be used on a large-scale study.

[1] A list of Members of the Consultative Committee is given on page 9.

## A Description of the Study

The authors of this present book are the research workers; their names and the sections on which they worked appear on pages 11 to 12. The method of organization whereby one person collects, analyses and presents the data for each area has both advantages and disadvantages which will not be enlarged upon here. It has meant that the sub-samples vary from section to section, as each research worker selected from the total of 59 those schools most appropriate for his investigation. Time, costs and other factors, such as the completion of the pupils' data also dictated the schools to be included in the various sections. The 59 schools in the study are described in detail later in this chapter. Thereafter, the book is divided into six sections, each reporting a part of the research that was undertaken in this more intensive fact-finding survey of comprehensive schools.

The six areas of study chosen for their particular relevances to a comprehensive system were:

1. patterns of school administration and organization and their effect on the teaching staff;

2. curricula and pupil welfare;

3. an attainment survey in reading, mathematics and non-verbal ability at the first- and fourth-year levels and an ability aptitude survey at the sixth-year level;

4. the extent to which mixing occurs between pupils of different social, ability and behaviour levels;

5. a survey of the organization of voluntary extra-curricular activities, and of the extent to which pupils of differing ages, abilities and social groups participate in them;

6. contacts and communication between the school and the parents and the school and the local community.

### What is a comprehensive school?

The objectives of comprehensive schools which distinguish them from other secondary schools, with which they have many aims in common, have been identified by a working party of educationalists as follows:

(i) 'to eliminate separation in post-primary education by gathering pupils of the whole ability-range in one school so that by their association pupils may benefit each other and that easy readjustments in grouping and in subjects studied may be made as pupils themselves change and develop';

19

(ii) 'to collect pupils representing a cross-section of society in one school, so that good academic and social standards, an integrated school society and a gradual contribution to an integrated community beyond the school may be developed out of this amalgam of varying abilities and social environments';

(iii) 'to concentrate teachers, accommodation and equipment so that pupils of all ability groups may be offered a wide variety of educational opportunity and that scarce resources may be used economically' (Monks, 1968).

In practice there are several types of comprehensive school. The Department of Education Circular 10/65 lists six main forms, although not all are acceptable as fully comprehensive. The orthodox school catering for all pupils between the ages of 11 and 18 is the most common type at present. In other types, the age range is limited and pupils may attend junior high or middle schools to 13 or 14 years and then move to senior schools. (If transfer is at 16 the senior school may be a sixth-form college). Other variations include schools for all pupils up to 13 or 14, and then either the transfer of *some* pupils to senior schools or a choice at that age between senior schools which run examination courses to 16 and 18 years and those which do not.

The schools included here are of all types with the exception of sixth-form colleges and middle schools which were not in existence at the time of the first survey.

### The sample of schools

Selection of a small sample of schools from the 331 included in the first stage of the study presented a number of problems: it was necessary to include not only schools representative of all types but also of many different authorities, for the problems of an urban or an Inner London Education Authority school are very different from those of a school in a rural area or new town. Other considerations of sampling were the sex of the pupils, the school's size and year of becoming fully developed as a comprehensive.

Since no sample could be fully representative, in a strict statistical sense, of the original very diverse population, a group of approximately 50 schools was regarded as the least that could be reasonably representative of the 222 which were fully developed in 1966/67. Several sections that follow are based on smaller sub-groups of the 59 schools. Limitations of personnel, time, costs and, in one instance the quality of the data dictated this: there is no reason to believe, however, that the findings reported here would have been altered in any way by these slight differences in sampling. For reasons of brevity, a statistical description of each sub-sample has been omitted from the beginning of each section.

TABLE 1.1: *Sample of schools related to year of becoming fully developed, size, and sex of pupils*

| TYPE OF SCHOOL | YEAR OF BECOMING FULLY DEVELOPED | | | | |
|---|---|---|---|---|---|
| | *1957 or Before* | *1958– 61* | *1962– 64* | *1965* | *Total* |
| *11–18* | 15 | 8 | 15 | 7 | 45 |
| *Other* | 2 | 1 | 1 | 10 | 14 |

| | NUMBER OF PUPILS ON ROLL | | | | | | | |
|---|---|---|---|---|---|---|---|---|
| | 600 | 601– 800 | 801– 1000 | 1001– 1200 | 1201– 1400 | 1401– 1600 | 1601– 1800 | 1801– 2000 | *Total* |
| *11–18* | 11 | 4 | 12 | 7 | 2 | 2 | 3 | 4 | 45 |
| *Other* | 7 | 4 | 2 | — | — | 1 | — | — | 14 |

| | SEX OF PUPILS | | | |
|---|---|---|---|---|
| | *Boys* | *Girls* | *Mixed* | *Total* |
| *11–18* | 5 | 8 | 32 | 45 |
| *Other* | 3 | 2 | 9 | 14 |

The 59 schools in the total sample, however, while being carefully selected from the 222 fully developed schools contacted in the first part of this study in terms of type, locality, size of intake and year of becoming fully developed, are not a truly random sample, for a few of the schools originally picked for inclusion in this second part of the study found themselves either unwilling or unable to spare the time for this research—some, indeed, because they were already taking part in other projects. Whilst this sample may therefore be regarded as adequately representative of the fully developed schools of the first survey in terms of the dimensions specified above, it probably gives a less satisfactory sample of comprehensive schools and comprehensive schooling as they exist today. For instance, although the number of comprehensive schools has considerably increased since the sample was drawn, the proportion of all-through 11-18 schools in the total has dropped slightly (see DES statistics).

Briefly, 45 of the 59 schools in the sample were of the orthodox 11-18 type and the remaining 14 catered for various sections of the pupils of secondary school age. Of the traditionally organized, one-third were fully established in 1957, the remainder becoming so over the following eight years with regard to the age-range of the pupils. The 14 'other type' schools not catering for the full age-range were on the whole more recently developed; only two of the 14 were established at or before 1957, while 10 became fully developed in 1965 (compared with seven of the 45 traditional schools).

The size of the schools varied greatly: of the 11-18 type, 11 of the 45 had fewer than 600 pupils. On the other hand, four had more than 1,800. The average size of these schools was somewhere between 800 and 1,000 pupils. The 'other type' schools of limited age-range were on average smaller; seven of the 14 schools had less than 600 pupils and only one more than 1,400. The majority of the schools in the samples were co-educational: 32 of the 45 orthodox were for both sexes, eight were for girls only and five for boys. Of the 'other type' schools, nine of the 14 were mixed, three were for boys and two for girls.

### The collection of information

The collection of information for this second part of the project began in Autumn 1967 and continued until Spring 1968, the research officers each organizing their own programmes and visiting the schools as necessary. For clarity, the sources of information and the method of its collection are listed below.

The following details were requested for each pupil: occupation of father, sex, ethnic origin, form, age, ability assessment and behaviour assessment. Each school was asked to supply copies of: the time table, curriculum details, departmental structures and staff lists.

Other data covering particular fields were also collected. The source of information and the method used to obtain it are listed below, the sections corresponding to the chapters in the book:

## A Description of the Study

| SOURCE | METHOD |
|---|---|
| *Administration: 50 schools: (Chapter 2)* <br> Head, deputy head, one or two senior staff (such as senior mistress, head of house, head of lower school), two heads of subject departments, two assistant teachers, five senior pupils (usually prefects) .. | Personal interview |
| *Curriculum and pupil welfare: 47 schools and intensive study of 19: (Chapter 3)* <br> Up to seven members of staff in each school covering the special responsibilities of timetabling, libraries, sixth forms, careers, settling down, guidance and counselling .. .. | Personal interview |
| *Attainments survey: 52 schools: (Chapter 4)* <br> First- and fourth-year pupils .. | NF68 (tests of reading, mathematics, non-verbal ability) |
| Sixth-year pupils .. .. .. | CP66 (tests of verbal and non-verbal ability) |
| *Sociometric study of friendship patterns: eight schools: (Chapter 5)* <br> All pupils .. .. .. .. | Questionnaire |
| *Extra-curricular activities: 31 schools and intensive study of 17: (Chapter 6)* <br> Heads .. .. .. .. <br> Pupils .. .. .. .. | Personal interview <br> Questionnaire |
| Also referred to briefly: <br> Pupil leaders .. .. .. <br> Teachers concerned with activities | Questionnaire <br> Questionnaire |
| *Contacts between the school and community: 47 schools: (Chapter 7)* <br> Heads .. .. .. .. | Questionnaire |

23

The schools took great trouble to provide all the information requested. The only difficulty was in getting the full data needed for the accurate classification of pupils. Although it was important for us to have details of parental occupations, it was equally important that pressure should not be applied in a sensitive area of inquiry. It was, therefore, specifically pointed out to heads of the schools that we were not asking for the pupils to be questioned; the information requested was only that probably already held in the schools. In the event, this proved inadequate in quantity and deficient in quality in a few schools and this particularly affected the number of schools that could be included in the sociometric and voluntary extra-curricular activity analyses.

As the chapters that follow are separate studies, their order is a matter of convenience only. The book has deliberately been kept as concise as possible and the tables published are only a few of the vast number produced. Readers interested in further details of the planning or tabulations should write to the National Foundation for Educational Research.

# CHAPTER TWO

# The Administration of Comprehensive Schools

## *by* A. W. BATES

THE Department of Education Circular 10/65 suggested that, wherever possible, an all-through comprehensive school should be at least six-form entry size so as to ensure a viable sixth form with a wide range of options for pupils.

The schools of the future are therefore likely to grow in size and, administratively, the problems of running them will probably increase, both because it will be necessary to provide teaching and adequate pastoral care for the very able as well as the remedial groups all under one roof, and because an increase in size brings its own problems.

For this study of administration 50 schools were included. It was decided to concentrate on teaching and general educational matters rather than routine office administration, building maintenance, etc., except where this encroached upon the duties of teachers. Since the possible extent of this overlap was not known in advance, administration was studied operationally, that is, by studying the actual work of teachers at various levels. For a number of reasons, the data for this were collected by personal interviews but, where relevant, other documentary evidence, such as that provided by timetables, was gathered. One member of the team spent one full day in each school, interviews being arranged with the head, deputy head, a maximum of two 'senior' staff, two heads of subject departments and two assistant teachers (with or without graded posts). A group of senior pupils was also seen. All interviews were structured and terms carefully defined but frequently it was necessary for teachers to enlarge upon certain points so that various school procedures could be explained. The chapter will therefore include sections on staffing, internal organization, the duties of senior staff, the varying activities of the classroom teacher and the administrative role of pupils.

## Staffing

The way in which any school is staffed is of obvious importance. The previous NFER survey examined the qualifications and experience of teachers in all comprehensive schools. Its main conclusion in this respect was:

> 'The overall information indicates that the teaching force at present employed (in comprehensive schools) is predominantly a well-qualified and experienced body.' (Monks, 1968).

The present survey confirmed the same basic staffing statistics of the original survey; indeed, the degree of similarity over the two years in the average figures is surprising. Teacher/pupil ratios in the 50 schools averaged 1:18 (the same as 1965/66) and, no doubt due to the operation of the quota system, showed little variation from school to school. The two main exceptions were junior high schools, with an average teacher/pupil ratio of 1:20, and schools in the London area, where the use of relatively large numbers of part-time staff reduced the ratio to 1:17. On average, just under one-fifth of the teaching in schools in the London area was done by part-time teachers (in two schools the proportion was as high as a quarter). The use of part-time teachers elsewhere was less (five per cent), but where they were used to any extent, this did not necessarily result in a reduced teacher/pupil ratio. The overall correlation between teacher/pupil ratio and the percentage of teaching done by part-time staff was $-0.29$.

The statistics for the turnover of staff between 1965/66 and 1967/68 were also similar; 15 per cent to 20 per cent of the full-time teachers were new to the schools each year. Turnover appeared to vary, however, more from school to school than did teacher/pupil ratio. The main factor associated with a higher than average rate of turnover was the ability of the pupils in the intake—in schools with relatively few (defined as less than 15 per cent) 'X'[1] or able children, the turnover rate was 20 per cent, compared with 14 per cent in those schools which had the expected number of 'X' pupils.

## Additional allowances

One of the main methods of attracting and retaining high quality staff, and hence a powerful instrument for determining the character of a school, is to offer additional staff salary allowances for posts of responsibility. The conditions under which these additional allowances are operated (together with the basic salary scales) are set out in what are commonly known as the Burnham Reports (DES, 1967; 1969). However, the Burnham Reports are guides rather than

---

[1] 'X' pupils are defined as 'Pupils well above average in general educational ability, i.e. approximately the top 20 per cent of a normal national distribution'.

binding documents on this subject. This means that the responsibility for the way in which head of department allowances in particular are used in individual schools lies very much with each local education authority. The magnitude of this responsibility can be judged from the fact that over £440,000 was spent on additional allowances in the 50 schools in the sub-sample in the academic year 1967/68. In other words, disregarding the latest increase in salaries in 1970, one would expect *additional* allowances in a comprehensive school of 1,000 pupils to be in the order of £10,000 per annum.

Both the 1967 and 1969 Burnham Reports determined statutorily that the number and value of graded posts *must* be related to the group number or unit total of each school, and *recommended* (but did not compel) local education authorities to relate head of department allowances to the group number or unit total of the school. The group number or unit total was determined both by the size of the school and by the age of the pupils. The units per pupil are set out as follows:

| Age of Pupil | No. of Units per Pupil |
| --- | --- |
| Under 13 years old    ..    ..    .. | 1 (1½ in 1969) |
| 13 years old but under 15    ..    .. | 2 |
| 15 years old but under 16    ..    .. | 4 |
| 16 years old but under 17    ..    .. | 6 |
| 17 years old or over    ..    ..    .. | 10 |

The group number was based on the unit totals. The 1967 agreement was in operation at the time of the survey. This was superseded by another report in 1969. While the value of the allowances were changed in 1969, the agreement was basically the same in principle, although there were a few important changes, referred to in this report where necessary. It will be seen that two schools of equal size but with varying numbers staying on, particularly into the upper sixth, would have widely different unit totals and therefore probably different group numbers. Consequently, if allowances were related solely to group number, one would expect more allowances in one school than the other.

A study was made into the way in which allowances were being given to, and distributed in, the 50 schools. For this part of the investigation, relating allowances received in the schools to various other factors, a points system was used. This was not evolved by us but was already in force in some local education authorities. It is a development of the unit score system laid down in the Burnham Report and is useful for making comparisons between schools. In this system, points are awarded for allowances as follows:

| Graded Post Scale | | | | Value 1967 | Value 1969 | Points |
|---|---|---|---|---|---|---|
| I | .. | .. | .. | £125 | £132 | 1 |
| II | .. | .. | .. | £210 | £222 | 2 |
| III | .. | .. | .. | £315 | £334 | 3 |

| Head of Department Grade | | | | Value 1967 | Value 1969 | Points |
|---|---|---|---|---|---|---|
| A | .. | .. | .. | £210 | £222 | 2 |
| B | .. | .. | .. | £315 | £334 | 3 |
| C | .. | .. | .. | £445 | £472 | 4 |
| D | .. | .. | .. | £570 | £604 | 5 |
| E | .. | .. | .. | £700 | £742 | 6 |

Allowances for senior masters or mistresses, where they were not head of a department, were calculated on the actual sum. Thus, a senior mistress allowance of £800 would count as seven points in 1967/68 (one point = approximately £112). Where the actual sum was not known, the allowance was calculated at four-fifths of the deputy head's allowance (the usual rate) and converted to points. The allowances of the heads and deputies have not been included because their allowances are fixed and not at the discretion of the local education authorities.

A points score was calculated for each school for the year 1967/68. Within a school, it was also possible to give a points score to various subject, pupil welfare and administrative responsibilities. This method gives an accurate picture of the responsibility allowances in each school and allows comparisons to be made both between schools and between various subject and other responsibilities.

Correlations were calculated between some school variables and these points scores:

    (a)   size of sixth forms ..     ..     ..     ..     $r = 0.73$
    (b)   group number     ..     ..     ..     ..     $r = 0.85$
    (c)   size of schools (without sixth forms)     ..     $r = 0.89$
    (d)   size of schools (all pupils)..     ..     ..     $r = 0.92$

The correlation with school size is surprisingly high, bearing in mind the great variety of schools and the fact that they were spread over 30 authorities.

Diagram 2·1 shows the relationship between the size of the school and number of allowance points. Although the correlation is high, some schools are located well away from the regression line. All except one of the junior and senior schools lie outside the limits of one standard error due to the weighting given to the age of the pupils in these schools. (The senior high school *below* the regression line had hardly any sixth-formers.) If the junior and senior high schools are removed, the equation for the regression line for the 42 all-through schools becomes:

$$y = 0.0782x + 6.98$$

and the standard error of the estimate 14·42. Put another way, the regression equation means roughly eight points for every 100 pupils, plus another seven points irrespective of the number of pupils. Approximately two-thirds of the 11-18 schools are within 14 points of their calculated figure. Thus, for example, one would expect about two-thirds of the schools with 1,000 pupils to have a points score lying between 70 and 100, i.e. $84 \pm 14$. In practice, in 1967/68 values this works out as a total allowance figure of between £8,000 and £11,200: each point being worth approximately £112.

This method of calculation is not, of course, the basis on which local education authorities calculate allowances, but it does reflect the way allowances were actually allocated in 1967/68.

Because the correlation between size of school and number of allowance points is so high, the regression equation could be useful. At the time of writing, no more than 25 per cent of secondary pupils attended comprehensive schools, but as more local education authorities reorganize their secondary education along comprehensive lines, problems arise of how to award allowances to the new schools. The regression equation could be used as a simple guide or yardstick to help determine the number of allowances for these new schools, providing they are all-through schools with an age-range of

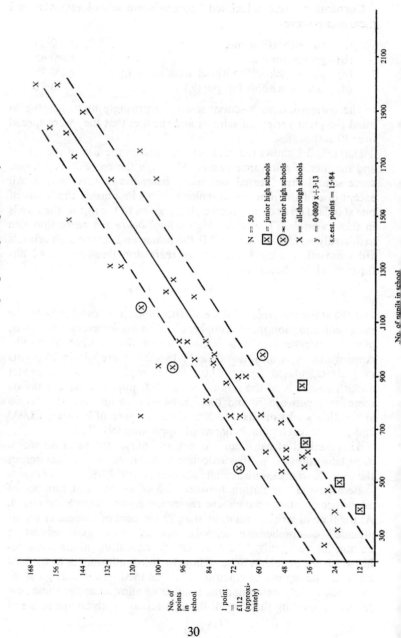

DIAGRAM 2.1: *Allowances for posts of responsibility*

No. of pupils in school

No. of points in school

1 point = £112 (approximately)

168
156
144
132
120
96
84
72
60
48
36
24
12

300 500 700 900 1100 1300 1500 1700 1900 2100

N = 50

⊠ = junior high schools
⊗ = senior high schools
X = all-through schools

y = 0·0809 x + 3·13

s.c.est. points = 15·84

11-18. (This is not to suggest, of course, that the formula should be applied blindly, but it might be used as a starting point for determining the number of allowances.)

## The distribution of allowances within the school

As important as the total amount of allowances awarded to a school is the way in which these allowances are used. The pattern of a school's allowance structure will reflect to some extent the school's priorities. The Burnham agreement is vague about the number of allowances a school may be given and vaguer still about their purpose; the relevant sections of the report are so worded that local education authorities have complete freedom in this. In this study, 30 of the 50 heads said they were given considerable freedom within the total to design the allowance structure in their own school and a further 10 heads appeared to have a fair degree of freedom.

The Table 2.1 shows the percentage distribution of allowances between the various kinds of responsibility of the schools.

TABLE 2.1 *The allocation of special allowances*

| RESPONSIBILITY | PERCENTAGE |
| --- | --- |
| Academic Subjects     ..     ..     ..     .. | 50 |
| Practical Subjects     ..     ..     ..     .. | 17 |
| Remedial/Less Able     ..     ..     .. | 3 |
| Other Subjects     ..     ..     ..     .. | 10 |
| Pupil Welfare and Administration..     .. | 20 |
| *Total %*     ..     ..     ..     ..     .. | 100 |

Almost half of the allowances for academic subjects went to mathematics and science posts: this means that almost one quarter of all allowances were for these posts while nearly one seventh were for those staff with house, year or head of lower, middle or upper school responsibilities.

The figures in the table are average figures; there were considerable variations between schools. For instance, in urban schools, particularly in the London area, a greater proportion of allowances was given to pupil welfare and administrative posts and less to academic (in London 42 per cent of allowances went to academic posts and the figure for all other urban schools was 51 per cent): in rural schools, on the other hand, more than 60 per cent was given to academic posts. Only a part of this tendency can be explained in terms of the size of school. The urban schools in the survey tended to be larger than the rural and, within broad limits, the bigger the school, the greater the proportion of allowances given to pupil welfare and administration. There was, however, considerable variation, so that not *all* large schools devoted a larger proportion of allowances to pupil welfare and administration than *all* the small and medium-sized schools (see Diagram 2·2).

Another important factor associated with the distribution of allowances was the proportion of 'X' or able pupils in the intake. When the proportion of 'X' pupils dropped below 15 per cent, the proportion of allowances for posts in academic subjects also decreased, while the proportion for pupil welfare and administration increased. There is, however, an important exception to this. Those schools partly or wholly of grammar school origin gave more allowances to academic subjects and fewer to pupil welfare and administration, remedial and practical subjects, even though their proportions of 'X' pupils were no higher than average.

Even in schools with low proportions of 'X' pupils there was a stronger emphasis on the use of allowances for academic posts if the school was derived from a grammar school. To some extent this may be due to the safeguarding of allowances for those teachers in the former grammar school remaining in the establishment after the reorganization. On the other hand, 12 of the 29 schools derived from grammar schools had been fully developed for at least 10 years at the time of the survey. This suggests that where a grammar school is changed into, or becomes a constituent part of, a comprehensive school, there is a strong tendency for the influence of the old grammar school to be long-lasting in the later structure of allowances.

It is not only in comprehensive schools derived from grammar schools that the influence of the bi-partite system is evident. The present Burnham agreement specifically emphasizes allowances for advanced work in subject departments, and recommends rewards for schools with many older pupils. The Burnham agreement as it stands is therefore geared primarily to reflect the needs of a bi-partite system. (This is perhaps to be expected, since at the time of the last agreement more than three-quarters of secondary pupils in State schools were still accommodated in such a system).

As far as comprehensive schools are concerned, the merit of the agreement is that with regard to allowances for posts of responsibility it is only a *guide* to local education authorities. From this survey

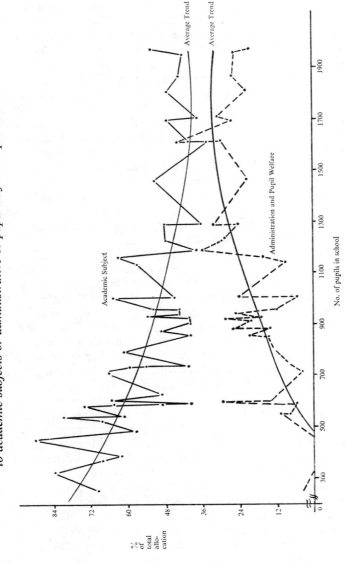

DIAGRAM 2.2: *Relationship between size of school and proportion of allowances given to academic subjects or administrative or pupil welfare responsibilities*

33

B

it would appear that local education authorities have in general attempted to fit allowances to the needs of their comprehensive schools, even if this has meant making arrangements not specifically covered by the Burnham agreement. For instance, the Burnham agreement makes no reference to the administrative demands of large schools, except to mention the possibility of allowances for 'teachers in charge of sections .... for example, lower school, middle school .... in large schools of, say, 1,000 pupils'.

However, there is nothing in the Burnham agreements to *prevent* such payments being made, and although there is no explicit reference to the possibility of allowances for house responsibilities, responsibilities for the less able, or for posts concerned with pupil welfare, such as careers advice or counselling, these posts alone accounted for almost 15 per cent of the money allocated for allowances in the schools surveyed. In half the small schools studied (less than 1,000 pupils) head of department or graded post allowances were used for house, or head of lower or middle school posts. Altogether, a quarter of the money for allowances went to 'non-subject' responsibilities in this study.

The major departure from a traditional interpretation of the Burnham agreement, however, was reflected in the increased emphasis given to the size of the school rather than the age of the pupils in determining the total allowances awarded. It could be argued that a system based on group numbers or unit totals and heavily influenced by the number in the sixth forms does not really meet the needs of comprehensive schools. The size of a sixth form is closely related to the quality of the pupil intake and therefore to the social make-up of the catchment area. A school in a 'poor' area usually has a low proportion of able pupils in the intake, and the number of such pupils staying on, particularly into the sixth, in relative terms, will drop still further due to economic factors. Under a traditional interpretation of the present Burnham agreement such a school would be penalized, since it would be awarded a lower unit total than a similarly sized school in a 'better' social area (even though an extra £75 is now payable to each qualified teacher in schools of exceptional difficulty). As allowances are supposedly related to the unit total, this would doubly penalize a school in a poor area. Such schools would be competing with those in 'better' areas for staff, yet would have fewer and less generous allowances to offer. In practice, since in this survey there was a negligible correlation ($r = 0\cdot08$) between the proportion of 'X' pupils and the number of allowances per pupil, local education authorities seemed generally to have awarded

34

allowances as much on the basis of the size of the school as on any other factor.

Some local education authorities in this study interpreted the Burnham agreement quite differently, and this led to a number of anomalies. For example, one rural all-through school, with approximately 700 pupils and a normal spread of ability in the intake, was awarded £13,000 in additional allowances in 1967/68—there were 12 Grade E posts, at that time each worth £700. These included Zoology and Latin department heads. Another rural all-through school of similar size, however, with the same number of pupils in the sixth form and the same spread of ability in the intake, was awarded only £8,000. There were two Grade E posts in this school, one each for English and Mathematics.

Anomalies are bound to occur when a considerable degree of freedom is allowed to local education authorities. Nevertheless, there may well be a case for the system of additional allowances in comprehensive schools to be reviewed. The possible advantages of using size alone as a criterion, at least for schools of similar age-range, and the need in large schools to use up to a quarter of their allowances for posts concerned with pupil welfare and administration, might well be considered in such a review. It is clear that the present Burnham agreement, while flexible, is being stretched to suit a comprehensive system, and the extent to which authorities are prepared to stretch the agreement also varies considerably.

### Internal organization

The organization of teaching (i.e. the grouping of pupils, the curriculum and the choice of subjects) is a fundamental concern of any school. This aspect of school organization will be described in Chapter 3. In this chapter the arrangements for dealing with the personal care of the pupils and their social problems are considered.

Any survey of this area of internal organization presents considerable problems, for the roles and responsibilities of the members of staff frequently overlap or are ill-defined, and a study of responsibility allowances is only one indicator of the school's organization and priorities. Also, the functions of similarly named organizational units may vary from school to school—for instance, a house may be no more than a means of providing competition in sport or it may be a miniature school within a school.

To illustrate the complexity of the interlocking systems and lines of communication that may exist in a school, it is perhaps worth quoting the case of an assistant geography teacher: he was a form master in the lower part of the school and also taught some forms in the upper. He was required to refer various matters to different members of staff as follows: matters concerning the academic progress of fifth-formers approaching entry for GCE 'O' level examinations, to the head of the geography department; those concerning persistent misbehaviour of a pupil in his registration form, to the head of the lower school; those concerning misbehaviour during a geography lesson of a fourth-former 'on report', to the housemaster; and those concerning advice on choice of subjects for a third-former wishing to take geography in the fourth year, but finding it clashed with other choices he had made, to the deputy head. This master was therefore involved in several channels of communication and different units of organization.

For this study of the relative importance of the various organizational units within the life of a school, an operational approach was adopted which tried to avoid over-simplification and to assess the strengths of the various units involved. This involved selecting specific activities concerned with pupil welfare and asking the head, deputy and senior staff which teachers were responsible for each. This operational picture of responsibilities was used in conjunction with other indicators of the strengths or importance of various organizational units. In this way, an index of the functional strength of each unit was built up in each school.[1] Generous financial allowances for house responsibilities, house-masters timetabled for comparatively few teaching periods and purpose-built accommodation for separate houses were, for instance, all seen as pointers to a strong house system.

Four alternative but in many cases interlocking organizational units cater for pupil welfare. These systems or units may be called the traditional, house, school and year systems.

*The Traditional System*

In the traditional system of organization pupil welfare is the responsibility of the head and the deputy head, helped in many cases by the senior master or mistress. This is the organization that would be expected in smaller schools. In this survey, however, it was found that even in the larger schools teachers in these 'traditional' posts continued to be involved to a considerable extent in pupil welfare. Nevertheless, in 26 of the 29 larger schools with more than 800 pupils, the school was divided in some way for the purposes of pupil

[1] For details of the scales, see Appendix B.

welfare, and in two-thirds of these larger schools the day-to-day handling of pupil welfare was clearly the responsibility of the sub-division. In contrast, 14 of the 21 smaller schools with less than 800 pupils were not divided to any extent and even where sub-divisions did exist, the traditional system usually dominated.

## The House System

At the start of this inquiry, it had been expected that when a school was sub-divided the house system would be the most prevalent form of organization. In this system, the school is grouped vertically so that each unit contains a cross-section of pupils of all ages. Perhaps on account of the functional approach adopted in this report, however, only 11 schools with strong house systems were identified and in three they were supplemented by some other form of organization. In another seven schools, the house system, while of functional importance, was secondary to other forms of organization. So no more than 18 schools, out of the total of 50, had a house system which was anything more than a nominal base for internal school competitions, assemblies or meals. This unexpectedly low figure is not due to the relatively large number of smaller schools, for the 11 schools with strong house systems were evenly spread over schools with from 600 to 1,800 pupils. Eight of these 11 schools were in purpose-built accommodation designed especially for comprehensive education, while in the remaining three, the majority of buildings had been added to convert an already existing school into a larger sized comprehensive school.

## The School and Year Systems

As common as a house system based on vertical grouping was the school system, with horizontal sub-divisions or units based on ages. Depending, of course, on the divisions, these units are usually termed 'lower', 'middle' and 'upper schools'. Seventeen schools in this study were sub-divided in this way. All were large, with more than 800 pupils. In other words, nearly 60 per cent of the larger schools were divided 'horizontally'. A system of age grouping was, therefore, more frequently found than house grouping in the larger schools.

Fourteen of the 17 schools had, at a minimum, a strong *lower* school sub-division, covering at least the first and second years; one other school was organized around three separate buildings and in the remaining two the responsibility of the year staff for welfare was no greater than that of the head, deputy and senior mistress. Staff responsible for lower, middle and upper schools (or school buildings) were generally given considerable autonomy in the day-to-day running of their sub-divisions.

Of the 15 schools with strong lower schools, 12 had been adapted, or had taken over a large proportion of their buildings, from previously existing schools. In 10 out of the 15, the school system was supplemented by some other form of organization. Often, this was a year system, where the welfare of all pupils in each school year was the direct responsibility of a particular teacher, who in most cases, at least in theory, would 'move up' each year, thereby remaining with the same group of pupils. In all seven schools with year systems this was not the major form of organization but was supplemented with some others: year systems were found in schools with widely differing building provision.

Apart from two small rural schools, each with about 50 boarding pupils, the arrangements discussed above covered all the schools in the survey. The use of the systems and their strength is summarized in Table 2.2.

TABLE 2.2: *The functional systems of organization for pupil welfare*

| Name of System | Number of Schools Where This System Was 'Strong' | Number of Schools Where This System Was Operative† |
|---|---|---|
| Traditional .. .. .. | 26 | 50 |
| House .. .. .. | 11 | 18 |
| School .. .. .. | 15 | 18 |
| Year .. .. .. .. | 2 | 7 |

† 'Operative'=responsible for at least some important aspects of pupil welfare.

It is apparent that both size and buildings determine to some considerable measure the organizational pattern of a school. When a school reaches about 800 pupils, it generally becomes too large for the traditional system alone to handle satisfactorily all the problems of pupil welfare. There are, however, certain practical difficulties in subdividing schools in the size range of 750 to 1,100 pupils. With the traditional four houses, or with at least five year groups, and with both boys and girls to be considered in mixed schools, a minimum of eight to 10 teachers, ideally, is required to head each organizational unit. This means that the number of allowances and extra 'free' periods that can reasonably be taken from the normal demands of subject teaching must be spread thinly in a school of this size. The effect of the thin spread of allowances and lack of 'free' periods is apparent in the 11 schools with house or year systems in this size-range. Only three had strong house or year systems and in two of these both the teacher/pupil ratio and the number of allowances were more generous than average.

One possible answer used and adapted in various ways by a few schools in this study was to concentrate a reduced teaching load and extra allowances on one or two positions. This was done by appointing a head of the lower school, in some cases assisted by a deputy, with the upper school remaining the direct responsibility of the head, deputy head and senior master or mistress. This arrangement particularly lends itself to schools in two separate buildings, whether on one site or not. The head of the lower school concentrates on the day-to-day problems of first- and second-years, looks after the settling down of the new pupils, makes contacts with primary schools and in general protects the interests of the younger pupils. In this study, five of the 14 schools in this size-range had lower school heads.

An alternative method, used by two of the smaller schools, was to create a head of the middle school, in charge of the third-, fourth- and fifth-years. The demands of pupils of this age for advice on choice of courses, examinations and careers can be considerable. A head of middle school is able to take responsibility for most of these matters, allowing the head, deputy head and senior master or mistress to concentrate on the first two years and the sixth form.

Once the size of the school reaches about 1,100 or 1,200 pupils size alone no longer restricts the adoption of various forms of organization. With teachers numbering 70 or more, the time and money required for eight or ten staff in charge of houses or years can be more readily absorbed from existing resources without this having a significant impact on subject priorities. The organization of the 16 largest schools in the survey reflects this. Among these were examples of strong systems with all variations of organization (traditional, house, school, year). Thus, above 1,200 pupils, size alone probably has little effect on *which* form of organization is adopted, compared with other factors such as the structure and situation of the school buildings.

Study of the data, together with knowledge gained from visiting the schools, indicates strongly that in all sizes of school the most important single factor influencing the form of organization adopted was the buildings, their situation and facilities. It is clear from this study that strong house systems are associated with purpose-built comprehensive schools, and school systems with adapted buildings. The influence of buildings in determining the form of organization has important consequences. Many, perhaps the majority, of the future comprehensives are likely to be adapted from or incorporate existing buildings.

The Department of Education and Science (1967) has set out some of the planning problems involved in converting buildings into comprehensive schools. Five case studies are examined and ten possible schemes outlined. In only one of these schemes could a satisfactory house system be established. The study by the Department of Education and Science complements the findings of this survey; both suggest that it has not usually been possible to organize a strong house system in schools adapted from existing buildings. If house systems are considered of educational value, it seems likely that they will only flourish in new, purpose-built comprehensive schools, or in adapted schools with considerable additions to the existing buildings.

### The duties of senior staff

With the structural organization of comprehensive schools outlined, a closer examination can be made of the day-to-day activities commonly carried out by senior members of staff.[1] These varied enormously both from school to school and from teacher to teacher, but in broad terms four major categories of activities other than teaching can be identified:

    (a)   planning for public examinations;
    (b)   arrangements for the welfare of pupils;
    (c)   general administration;
    (d)   planning the curriculum.

Before expanding those four categories, however, the teaching load of senior staff must be considered.

### Teaching

In even the largest schools, senior staff were usually involved in classroom teaching and most were timetabled to teach for a minimum of 10 periods a week. Marking and lesson preparation also

[1] 'Senior staff' normally includes heads, deputies, senior masters and mistresses and heads of school divisions, where these play an important part in the organizational structure of the school.

averaged over five hours a week—little different from the average eight hours a week for heads of subject departments and assistant teachers. Senior staff lost approximately the equivalent of one period a week from their scheduled timetables due to interruptions and other engagements, and they spent the equivalent of almost one period a week filling in for absent staff. Deputy heads and heads of school sections tended to lose more time from interruptions than did other levels of staff, and deputy heads also tended to spend more time than their colleagues filling in for absent staff. It was clear that even in the largest comprehensive schools, senior staff did a considerable amount of classroom teaching.

The main exceptions to this generalization were the heads, who did little classroom tuition and deputy heads who in the largest schools generally taught more and did more marking and lesson preparation than heads in the smallest schools in the survey. Thirteen heads were not timetabled to teach at all, while only two spent more than four hours a week, and nearly half no time at all, on marking and lesson preparation. In fact, the amount of time heads of school sections spent on marking and lesson preparation rarely exceeded four hours per week. This, contrary to the general tendency with other levels of staff, did not increase significantly with the number of lessons taught.

These tendencies suggest that in some schools deputies and heads of school sections may be over-timetabled, and time which would normally be spent on teaching activities is having to be sacrificed to other duties. Not unexpectedly, it was found that senior staff were scheduled to teach more periods in the smaller than in the larger schools. This generalization, however, does not hold for the heads of houses and years—these members of staff were timetabled for approximately 26 periods a week, irrespective of the size of the school.

We go on now to look at the four categories listed above.

### 1. *Planning for Public Examinations*

From inquiries made about preparing pupils for public examinations, it became apparent that six main administrative processes are involved.

(a) For most subjects the decision on type of examination (GCE, CSE, RSA, etc.) had to be made when the pupils were in their third year and reviewed towards the end of their fifth year.

(b) Before the final date for submitting entries to the examining boards, subject teachers named those pupils whom they considered to be suitably prepared. In only three schools in this study were all pupils, once accepted on a course, automatically entered for the examination.

(c) In 14 out of the 47 senior high and 11-18 schools entering pupils for public examinations, all or nearly all the pupils wishing to enter were interviewed by one or more senior members of staff. In the remaining 33, however, pupils were seen only when problems arose. These problems were usually dealt with on an *ad hoc* basis, whoever happened to be available dealing with the matter since the responsibility for this was generally shared.

(d) All heads bear the ultimate responsibility of which pupils may be entered, though they may not actually make the decision themselves. In this study, in only 15 of the 44 schools for which information was available was the head actively involved in this decision, and these schools tended to be the smaller ones.

(e) The responsibility for the routine administration of examinations in most schools fell on the shoulders of the deputy head; 37 of the 47 deputy heads were involved to a considerable degree in the routine administration of both public and internal examinations in their schools.

(f) About half of the schools gave their pupils every opportunity to re-sit 'O' level examinations if they wished to do so; in one school only (a junior school) were pupils not allowed to re-sit 'O' levels, while in another, pupils were not allowed to re-sit 'O' levels unless they were considered suitable 'A' level candidates. In the remaining schools, there was a screening procedure by senior staff, but it is not known how rigorous this was.

## 2. *Arrangements for the General Welfare of Pupils*

This section is concerned with the direct contacts between senior staff and pupils. The variety of welfare activities to emerge under this general heading was considerable.

(a) *Choice of courses.* It could be argued that in a comprehensive educational system, one of the most important decisions for all pupils and their families is which subjects or course to study. In 20 of the 48 schools for which adequate information was available, every pupil was interviewed individually about choice of subjects by some senior member of staff. This was more likely to occur in those schools with strong sub-divisions than in those not sub-divided, or only weakly so. Nevertheless, in 15 of the remaining 28 schools, it was reported that such interviewing was the responsibility of subject or form teachers, only problems being referred to the more senior level. The overall impression, however, was that in most of these 28 schools there was a lack of clarity about whose responsibility it was to advise pupils—or even if *individual* advice to pupils on choice of subject was a responsibility of the school. Certainly, in some schools it did not seem to be considered important.

In all but three of the schools for which information was available and relevant at least one member of staff was specifically responsible for careers advice. In 27 schools additional salary allowances were specified for this responsibility—these were more common in urban than in rural areas. Career advice and guidance will be enlarged upon in the following chapter.

(b) *Interviewing parents*. All teachers interviewed were asked about the number of parents they saw individually in a normal week. Excluding contacts made on parents' evenings or similar occasions and fleeting contacts such as receiving a message that a pupil was sick, these individual contacts between parent and teacher were extremely rare. Formal arrangements for asking parents to the school are therefore all the more important.

The number of parents seen individually by heads remained roughly the same at about half a dozen a week, irrespective of the size of the school, the extra interviewing as schools increased in size being delegated to the staff in charge of the various sub-divisions of the school. Even so, heads generally saw more parents than did any other individual member of staff in their schools, except possibly the heads of school sections.

(c) *Report writing*. In contrast to seeing parents, staff at all levels were involved to a considerable extent with written reports to parents. Reports were sent home at least once a year in every school in the sample and in the great majority this was done twice a year. In schools with up to 1,000 pupils, the head usually checked end-of-term reports for all the pupils in the school without assistance from other staff, but even in the larger schools the head was generally involved in checking at least some. It is not surprising, therefore, that a substantial proportion of senior staff, about a third of the heads, and half the heads of school sections and houses, estimated that they spent over 25 hours a year on checking or writing end-of-term reports. Indeed, three heads and one head of a school section said they spent over 100 hours a year on this alone.

Over three-quarters of the heads were involved in writing testimonials for pupils wishing to continue in further or higher education and this may partly explain the commitment of the heads to end-of-term report writing in even the largest schools. For testimonials to employers, however, only just over half the heads were involved; this is paralleled by a corresponding increase in the commitment of other senior staff, particularly the heads of houses. In general, heads seemed very reluctant to delegate all checking of reports and the writing of testimonials.

(d) *The reception of new pupils.* The responsibilities of senior staff for the reception of new pupils varied considerably. Senior staff from 15 schools in the survey visited primary schools to see and talk to prospective pupils; 20 schools held meetings for parents of new pupils; 20 ensured that every new pupil was interviewed by at least one senior member of staff. In only four schools, on the other hand, were no specific arrangements made for seeing new pupils or their parents. Pupils were more likely to be individually interviewed if their school was strongly sub-divided. It is possible, however, that the interviewing of new pupils is bound up with selection at 11-plus, since it was more frequent in schools where pupils underwent a selection procedure. Indeed, in all London schools, all new pupils were interviewed individually.

(e) *Provision for sick pupils.* Thirteen of the schools in the survey, most of which were large, had matrons or nurses to look after sick pupils. In others, it was the senior mistress who was generally responsible. In large schools without a matron, the senior mistress would see perhaps somewhere between 30 and 50 sick pupils per week.

Although it is not possible to cover all the activities of teachers with regard to pupil welfare, it is possible to identify some general tendencies. Few areas of pupil welfare were completely delegated by heads. Instead, heads tended to share these activities as their duties increased. Basically, there was a perceptible reluctance on the part of the heads to break with the main sources of direct contact with pupils and, probably related to this, there appeared in many of the schools to be a lack of clear delegation of responsibilities. Problems tended to be dealt with if and when they arose by whoever was available at the time. It is interesting to note, therefore, that in schools with strong sub-divisions (and therefore generally the large schools) there was a greater probability that *all* pupils would be individually interviewed by senior staff regarding choice of courses, careers and entry to the school. Finally, a considerable amount of time appeared to be spent by all levels of staff on written reports to parents, but, in contrast, contacts with parents, except in 'formal' parents' evenings, were sparse.

### 3. General Administration

To ensure a balanced picture of the work of senior staff, the interviewer also asked about arrangements for staff absences, contacts with professional workers from outside the school (school doctors, probation officers, etc.), committee work, and visitors. Deputy heads normally arranged for cover for absent staff, although where there was a head of a 'school' section he was also likely to be involved.

In one large school, a senior member of staff was in charge of student teachers, with an additional allowance for this responsibility; in another large school, an honorarium was paid by the local university school of education to teachers in the school to act as as tutors for student teachers. The head's main contact with an outside professional worker was most likely to be with the probation officer, but the most frequent visitor was the youth employment officer, who visited all but three of the schools with fourth-year leavers.

Some heads of schools spent a large proportion of their time on outside committee work and with visitors to the school. Their schools were usually large and situated in the south of England, although they were not exclusively in London. In some cases, heads averaged at least 10 hours a week on these activities. One head said that visitors alone accounted for about 30 per cent of his time; another reported having 66 parties of visitors, 296 people altogether, in one term alone—none of whom had been initially invited by the school. One head had proposed to his local education authority that a full-time public relations officer should be appointed to the school to deal with visitors and requests for information, and several schools had of necessity strictly limited the number of visitors.

### 4. Planning the Curriculum

Planning the curriculum is generally not a major problem in small schools, where contact between all teachers is relatively easy and frequent, and where the range of subjects offered is more limited, nor is it such a task in schools with a fairly homogeneous intake of pupils. In large comprehensive schools, however, planning the curriculum is a major administrative problem, for a wide range of differing, sometimes competing, objectives must be reconciled. The number of teachers may exceed 100, making communication difficult, yet the decisions reached must, as far as possible, suit the needs of pupils of all types. It is therefore as important to know *how* policy decisions are reached as to know *what* these decisions are (curriculum content is discussed in Chapter 3). What follows is an attempt to structure the process of curriculum decisions, based on discussions with the members of staff most concerned with the construction of the timetable in each school.

In a few schools, mention was made of a curriculum study group or a working party concerned with curriculum development. In most schools, it was clearly the head who had the final word on curriculum policy, but other levels of staff were involved in the final policy decision in some schools and in only two schools were the major policy decisions on curriculum made by the deputy head and senior master respectively. The majority of heads of subject departments were, however, asked to suggest how staff in their department should be deployed.

Seven of the eight schools where the timetable was compiled during the summer holidays were small schools. The difficulty appeared to be that during term time deputy heads were heavily committed to teaching and the heads had many other responsibilities which meant that there was insufficient time for work on the time-table. The compilation of the timetable was usually carried out by the deputy head, although heads were involved in about a third of the smaller schools. In the majority of schools, including large schools, the timetable was compiled by one person.

## A General Picture of the Duties of Senior Staff

It was rare for any level of staff, other than the head, to teach for less than a third of the timetable. Teachers in charge of houses and years, in even the largest schools, were generally as heavily time-tabled as heads of subject departments. It is not surprising, therefore, that these results indicate a need for senior staff to have sufficient time free from classroom teaching to undertake other duties.

Related to this was the emergence of the heads of school sections as powerful figures in school administration. Particularly where schools were on separate sites, the section head's responsibilities were exceeded only by the head's himself. He was generally less involved with class instruction than any level of staff other than the head and deputy. A head of school section usually dealt directly with parents and would see almost as many each week as the head. However, perhaps because of the size of the unit for which they were responsible, heads of school sections were less likely than house staff to give individual advice to *each* pupil in their section on careers and choice of courses, although within a lower or middle school unit year staff were sometimes given this responsibility. It was certainly true that continuity of advice was more likely in schools with strong house systems, help with choice of courses and advice on careers being given usually by the same person (the housemaster or mistress) which was generally not the case in schools with horizontal organizations. Nevertheless, it was clearly more likely that individual advice to every pupil would be given by senior staff in schools that were sub-divided, either vertically or horizontally, than in schools which were not sub-divided.

The survey also showed the importance of the deputy head in the administration of medium-sized schools. The deputy heads in medium-sized schools were generally more involved in a wide range of activities than deputy heads in large or small schools. It was not clear whether this was due to the difficulty of sub-dividing schools into sufficiently 'strong' smaller units in this size-range or whether it was due to a limited number of activities taking up more of the deputy head's time in large schools.

It is clear that administration within the schools in the survey is highly individual, depending on the personal inclinations of the staff and especially the head. In many instances, the impression was that problems were tackled as they arose, on an *ad hoc* basis. Often there was no clear delegation of responsibility for various activities, or responsibility was shared between several members of staff. It was also noticeable that heads of large schools were reluctant to relinquish their main contacts with pupils, although the main responsibility for individual pupil welfare lay, at least in theory, with the heads of school sub-divisions. It was, in fact, difficult to identify activities carried out by heads of large schools that were not also carried out by heads of medium-sized and small schools although, of course, the amount of time spent on each activity differed considerably with size.

In several schools, because of the tendency to deal with problems as they arose and perhaps also because duties were not always clearly delegated, senior staff, particularly the head, were often under considerable pressure to cope with what seemed an almost constant flow of 'day-to-day' and comparatively minor problems.

### The 'classroom' teacher

In an attempt to find out how the way a comprehensive school is organized affects the work of 'classroom' teachers, teachers were asked to estimate how much time they spent on various activities. 'Classroom' teachers were defined as heads of subject departments, assistant teachers without graded posts and those with graded posts who were not in charge of house or year groups, unless these units were functionally weak.

Three or four classroom teachers were interviewed in each school, making a total of 187 covering the full range of subjects and experience. The teachers interviewed were not strictly a representative sample of all classroom teachers in comprehensive schools, for a relatively high proportion of heads of subject departments were seen. However, since teacher variables were similarly distributed between the different kinds of school (e.g. approximately the same proportion of graduates was interviewed in large as in small schools) statements made about differences between kinds of school can be assumed to be valid. On the other hand, one is probably less justified in making statements about 'average' figures for teachers' activities.

On the basis of a pilot study, a list of the main activities carried out by classroom teachers was drawn up. The 53 items were grouped into the following nine sections:

*Instruction.* Time spent on class instruction; lesson preparation; marking, except exams; room readinesss; filling in for absent staff; teacher supervision.

*Pupil welfare.* Discussing pupils' problems with pupils themselves, with parents individually, at public meetings and with staff; discipline; detention.

*Records of pupils.* Formal reports; record sheets; school exams—setting, marking and supervision.

*Clerical duties.* Registration; collecting dinner and other money; stocktaking (in and out of school time); returns to education office; external examination arrangements; ordering and obtaining stationary; duplicating.

*Policy.* Staff-meetings; large-scale building provision; ordering books and/or equipment; work on syllabus; making or helping with staff appointments; school timetables; staff welfare and grievances; transfer of pupils between forms.

*Extra-curricular activities.* Clubs and societies; making arrangements; school social functions; school journeys (in and out of school time).

*Supervision.* Public exams; playgrounds; buildings; meals; library; games (out of school time); allocation and supervision of prefect duties.

*Outside contacts.* Representation of school at public meetings, etc.; CSE, GCE, and subject meetings; organizing and attending courses (in and out of school time); visitors.

*Miscellaneous.* Assembly; waiting around; movement; caretaking.

All these activities were defined for each teacher at the interview, and they were asked to estimate the amount of time spent on each. Although the estimates were approximate, considerable differences were found in the various types of school, possibly indicating a relationship between type of school and the activities of classroom teachers.

The individual estimates were added to give a total for each teacher. These figures should clearly be treated with caution, since we know from other investigations that such estimates are less than totally reliable. Diagram 2.3 shows the distribution of total times for the 187 teachers. The mean or average was 43 hours a week, with a standard deviation of approximately eight hours, with the distribution slightly skewed towards the lower end. Since the length of the school day sets a minimum limit, this is what one would expect. The smallest estimate was just under 27 hours a week: the largest 71 hours! The estimates for almost a fifth of the teachers exceeded 50 hours a week, but on the other hand, for another fifth, they fell below 36 hours.

Of the 10 school variables (age-range, sex, size of school, size of sixth form, origin, region, urban/rural location, number of years fully developed, percentage of 'X' pupils, split or single-site buildings) and the six teacher variables (main subject taught, sex, qualifications, experience, level of appointment, whether form teacher or not), the major factors significantly related to a longer working week were: size of school; subject taught and the qualifications of the teacher.

Large schools appeared to demand slightly more time from their teachers, and it is they that are principally responsible for the significant association found between size and the average number of hours worked. In spite of this association, however, there were of course many teachers in small schools who worked longer hours than many in large.

DIAGRAM 2.3: *Total of estimates (in hours) for 'classroom' teachers' activities*

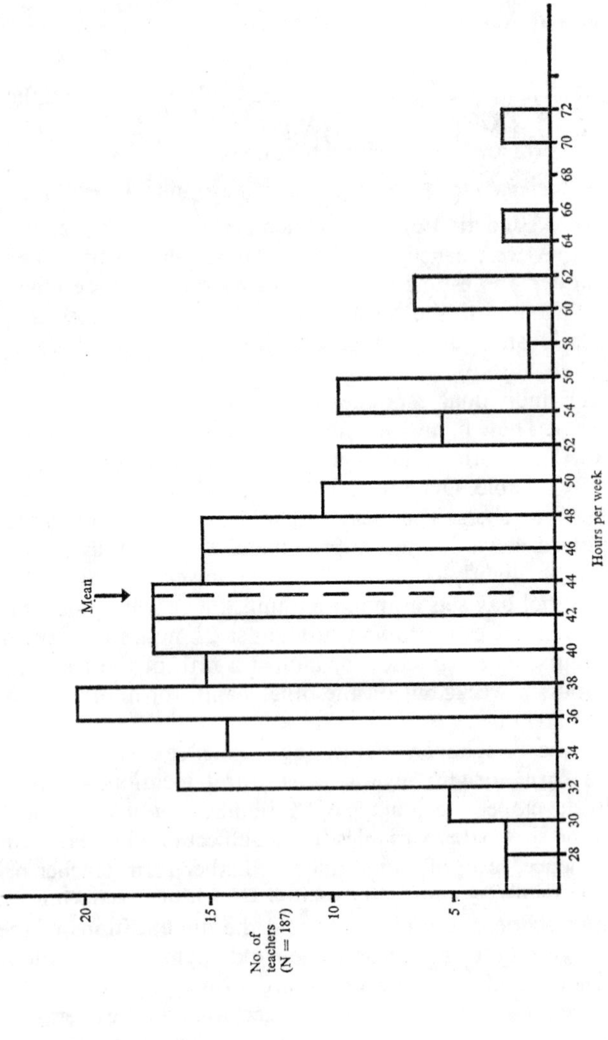

Staff teaching English, Modern Languages, History and Geography had longer working hours than those in other departments. The English teachers averaged approximately 46½ hours per week, the Modern Language one hour less and the History and Geography staff almost 44. These compare with just over 41 hours for the mathematicians and 37 for those teaching practical subjects. The total hours worked by those in other departments were intermediate. Lighter marking and lesson preparation requirements mainly accounted for these differences.

TABLE 2.3: *Size of school and hours worked by classroom teachers*

| No. of Schools | Size of School | No. of Teachers Interviewed | Mean | | SD | |
|---|---|---|---|---|---|---|
| | | | *Hrs.* | *Mins.* | *Hrs.* | *Mins.* |
| 20 | <751 | 73 | 41 | 23 | 7 | 48 |
| 18 | 751–1250 | 74 | 42 | 59 | 7 | 18 |
| 12 | 1251 or more | 40 | 45 | 30 | 9 | 32 |

F ratio$=3\cdot29$, $p<0\cdot05$

The number of hours worked by graduates was almost four hours more than those worked by non-graduates: nearly 44½ hours a week compared with just over 40½. This, once again, is largely explained by the more exacting demands of lesson preparation and marking of the subjects most frequently taught by graduates.

Apart from size of school, the total estimated working time of classroom teachers in each school was not related to the other school variables.

*Within* this total working time, however, school variables were influential in the deployment of teachers' time. Relatively more time was spent on activities concerned with pupil welfare and less on subject teaching in certain kinds of school. This conclusion was reached by comparing the amount of time spent on 'subject directed' activities (class instruction, lesson preparation, marking and examinations) with time spent on activities that were 'welfare directed' (including pupil welfare, contacts with parents, extra-curricular activities, journeys abroad, visits to factories). Significant differences are associated with three of the main variables: size of school, urban or rural location and region.

Teachers spent on average nearly one hour more on welfare-directed activities and over one hour less teaching in the large than in the small schools. Similarly, teachers in London and other urban areas spent, on average, respectively one and a half and one hour more on welfare directed activities and two and a half and one hours less on subject directed activities than teachers in rural areas. A breakdown by region showed that teachers in schools in the south spent the least amount of time on teaching and the most on welfare activities. Compared with teachers in Wales, the south averaged four hours less teaching and three hours more on welfare. Between these two extremes were the teachers in the northern and midland regions.

Large schools in this survey, however, were generally those in densely-populated areas, and differences related to the size of the school may merely reflect geographical or social factors which, in turn, may be associated with both differences in teacher attitudes and varying pupil needs.

Calculations were made on the actual amount of lesson time scheduled for pupils. The most common arrangement found in 15 schools was 35 periods a week of 40 minutes each, that is 23 hours 20 minutes a week. Another six schools had 40 periods of 35 minutes a week, giving the same teaching time. In the remaining 29 schools 18 different timing arrangements were found with the total lesson time per week varying from 22 hours 5 minutes to 26 hours 40 minutes. Between these two extremes there is a difference of seven weeks per year, or almost a whole school year over a period of six years. However, comprehensive schools are not exceptional in showing such wide variations, for the Department of Education and Science (1968) in a survey of secondary schools, found that: 'The actual number of minutes of the normal timetable cycle varied considerably between schools'.

The results of the two surveys are similar, as Table 2.4 shows.

Schools of certain types were likely to have a longer day scheduled for lessons. Pupils in Wales received on average 90 minutes a week more time on lessons than pupils in either the south or north of England, but pupils in the midlands were also more heavily scheduled, by up to an hour, than those in other parts of England. There also appeared to be some relationship between the origin of the school and the amount of time scheduled. Schools derived from grammar schools averaged an hour per week more than new schools or those derived solely from secondary modern schools. Further, the five schools with relatively high proportions of 'X' or able pupils averaged nearly an hour more per week than others in the survey. Obviously, the higher the proportion of able pupils the more the scheduled lesson time.

TABLE 2.4: *Number of minutes in the timetable cycle*

| Source | No. of Schools | <1400 | 1400–1500 | 1500–1600 | 1600–2000 | 2000 and Over |
|--------|----------------|-------|-----------|-----------|-----------|---------------|
| DES | 435 | 9·4% | 58·0% | 17·9% | 8·7% | 6·0% |
| NFER | 50 | 6·0% | 66·0% | 22·0% | 6·0% | 0% |

The findings discussed for classroom teachers in conjunction with those presented for the pupils' scheduled lesson time suggest that, in comprehensive schools in more difficult social areas (the large urban schools and those with relatively few able pupils), less time is devoted to subject-directed activities and more to welfare-directed activities. It could be argued that pupils in schools in less favourable areas should receive at least as much, if not more time for lessons as those in the more favourable areas, but an increase in one kind of activity seems to be associated with a decrease in another which would appear equally vital to the well-being of the pupils and the school community.

### The role of pupils in school administration

All but one school in the survey had prefects or senior pupils; nearly all had a head boy and/or girl, and in most there were also deputies, house or sub-prefects. In addition, roughly three-quarters of the schools had form-captains. The average proportion of pupils per school who were intermediate or full prefects at any one time was 10 per cent. Half the schools in the survey had school councils, and just under half prefects' councils and/or sixth form societies. In fact, only six schools had none of these representative bodies or societies.

Pupils usually chose their own form captains and school council members, but the sixth-form societies were usually open to all those eligible. In about one-third of the schools sixth-formers automatically became prefects or were elected by pupils; these systems may be termed 'non-élitist' prefect systems. In other schools, pupils in positions of responsibility were chosen by the head or by the head and teachers. At all levels of pupil responsibility, the main duties were supervision of other pupils, and assistance to teachers in the day-to-day running of the school. In a quarter of the schools, however, prefects were expected to take responsibility for organizing or carrying out a wide range of welfare activities. There was little evidence of pupil involvement in school policy-making, although in half, school councils provided an opportunity for grievances or suggestions to be aired.

Although statistical analysis has been unpracticable in many instances because of the small number of schools involved, organizational factors do seem to be linked to differences in pupil responsibilities and administration. Large schools, and/or those in the south, particularly London were more likely to have school councils and sixth-form societies, and to expect their prefects to take responsibility for welfare activities. Their prefect systems were also more often 'non-élitist'. On the other hand, school councils were less frequently found in Wales or in schools of grammar origin, but prefects' councils were more likely to be in schools with large sixth forms. Single-sex schools, those with low proportions of 'X' or able pupils and those derived from secondary modern schools were more likely to have sixth-form societies, although these were not common in the midland schools.

Attitudes towards the role of pupils in school administration seem to vary from school to school, but generally opportunities exist through school councils or prefects' councils for pupils to raise important matters. It was not possible from this study to say whether pupils were encouraged to discuss matters of school organization and policy. It is apparent, however, that some comprehensive schools have rejected a traditional 'élitist' approach to pupil responsibility although it is not yet clear what will emerge in its place.

**Summary**

The diversity of schools in this sample of 50 reflected the variety of comprehensive schools generally. This diversity is a direct result of decisions taken by both central and local government. It is hardly surprising, therefore, that *within* the schools there was an enormous range of administrative practice. Consequently, for every generalization made there will usually be many exceptions. The findings of this chapter follow.

1. The teacher/pupil ratio, with little variation, was 1:18. Apart from the London area, part-time staff formed a very small proportion of the teaching force, constituting about seven per cent of the staffing (Appendix Table A2.1).

2. The turnover of full-time teachers was about 15 per cent to 20 per cent per annum. Both the teacher/pupil ratio and the percentage turnover of staff were almost the same in 1967/68 as they were two years earlier.

3. Additional allowances for posts of responsibility (excluding the head and deputy head) averaged eight points for every 100 pupils in the schools, plus another seven points irrespective of size of school, with a standard error of $\pm$ 14 points. On 1967/68 values, each point was worth approximately £112. Between £400,000 and £450,000, or almost £10 for every pupil, was spent on allowances for posts of responsibility (excluding the head and deputy head) in 1967/68 in the 50 schools in the survey.

4. Fifty per cent of the additional allowances were allocated to academic subject responsibilities, 20 per cent to administrative or pupil welfare responsibilities and the remaining 30 per cent to non-academic subjects. Twenty-five per cent of the total went to mathematics and science posts.

5. Local education authorities in general seem to have fitted allowances to the needs of comprehensive schools, although this has frequently meant making arrangements not covered by the Burnham agreement. Many anomalies were found in the interpretation of the Burnham agreement regarding allowances.

6. By basing allowances for posts of responsibility on unit totals, strict adherence to the principles of the present Burnham agreement would result in penalizing comprehensive schools in poor areas. This is because they would receive fewer extra allowance points per pupil, since a smaller proportion of their older pupils stay on after the minimum school leaving age.

7. The 'traditional' system of organization whereby pupil welfare and administration are the direct responsibility of the head, deputy head and senior master or mistress was evident in all schools. Over half the schools in the survey had less than 1,000 pupils and in the majority of these the traditional system was the major form of organization. When the size of school exceeded 750 to 800 pupils, however, the traditional system was generally supplemented to a considerable degree by some other organizational system.

8. Strong house systems were found in just under a quarter of the schools; they were usually in schools which were purpose-built or those largely rebuilt as comprehensive schools.

9. Strong 'school' systems (lower, middle, upper school sections) operated in about a third of the schools; they were usually found in schools adapted from existing buildings. Schools with strong 'school' systems usually adopted a further form of sub-division, such as year-groups.

10. Year systems were found in 14 per cent of the schools in the survey, but were seldom the major organizational unit in a school.

11. In many schools, organization was complex. In a quarter of the schools assistant teachers were part of (and responsible to) at least four separate organizational units (e.g. traditional, subject, house, lower school).

12. The major factors influencing the form of school organization appeared to be the size of the school and the form and disposition of its buildings.

13. Schools of medium size (750 to 1,250 pupils) appeared to have special difficulties in forming strong sub-divisional units. Several possible arrangements were discussed.

14. Apart from head teachers in large schools, senior staff were heavily involved with classroom work. Most senior staff, even in large schools, taught for over a third of the available time and spent at least six hours a week on marking and lesson preparation. In some schools, there were indications that deputy heads and heads of school sections, given their other responsibilities, were over-timetabled for teaching (Appendix Table A2.2).

15. Six main administrative procedures in the preparation of pupils for public examinations were identified: (a) choice of course of subjects, including the type of examination for which the pupils will study; (b) recommendations for entry; (c) review of each pupil's overall commitment; (d) final decision on which subjects a pupil will be entered for; (e) routine examination administration; (f) resit arrangements.

16. In just under half of the schools in the survey, each pupil was interviewed individually about choice of subjects by some senior member of staff. This occurred more frequently in those schools that were strongly sub-divided, in other words, in the larger schools.

17. A member of staff was responsible for careers advice in all

schools with fourth-year leavers and in three-fifths of these there was an allowance or allowances for this responsibility. Careers advice was more likely to be given to sixth-formers by the most senior levels of staff and to fourth- and fifth-formers by careers teachers.

18. Careers advice was generally given by careers teachers or specialists (e.g. youth employment officer) after choice of subjects or course had been made and except in schools with strong house systems, advice on careers tended to be given by different teachers from those who gave advice on choice of subjects.

19. Other than through formal parents' evenings, etc. when large numbers of parents generally attended, individual 'private' contacts between teachers and parents were rare. Forty-eight per cent of the classroom teachers interviewed had no contact of this kind with parents.

20. About a third of the head teachers and half the heads of school sections and heads of houses spent over 25 hours a year on writing and checking reports for parents. Classroom teachers averaged about 15 to 20 hours a year each on reports.

21. In two-fifths of the schools, each pupil in the new intake was interviewed individually by some senior member of staff. This was more likely to occur in schools that were strongly sub-divided, and therefore in larger schools.

22. One quarter of the schools had matrons or nurses. These appointments were mainly in schools with more than 1,250 pupils.

23. Few areas of pupil welfare were delegated completely by heads to other levels of staff. As schools increased in size, one or two of the heads' activities were dropped and more were shared with other levels of staff, but basically there was a perceptible reluctance on the part of heads to break with the main sources of direct contact with pupils.

24. There appeared to be a lack of clear delegation of responsibility for several of the activities examined in many schools. Problems were dealt with if and when they arose by whoever was available at the time. In many schools, administration was highly individualized, determined in some considerable degree by the personality of the teachers and the inclinations of the head.

25. In a small number of schools in the survey, a large proportion of the head's time (10 hours a week or more) was devoted to visitors and committee work.

26. Where this position existed, heads of school sections appeared to be important figures in school administration. In some schools their responsibilities were exceeded only by those of the head. Deputy heads in medium-sized schools also appeared to carry a wide range of responsibilities.

27. The usual amount of time scheduled for teaching was between 23 and 25 hours per week, but this varied considerably. In some schools, pupils were timetabled for over 150 hours a year more than pupils in other schools.

28. Sixty per cent of the classroom teachers interviewed gave estimates of activities totalling between 36 hours and 50 hours a week. The mean was 43 hours a week.

29. Large schools tended to demand slightly more time of their staffs. Teachers in large schools and those in urban areas (particularly London) gave a greater proportion of their time to activities concerned with pupil welfare and less to subject teaching than their colleagues in rural or small schools (Appendix Table A2.3).

30. Although specific activities of teachers are clearly influenced by organizational factors, these alone do not explain the wide differences between teachers. Apart from factors such as the subject taught, probably as important in influencing the activities of teachers are the predominating home backgrounds of the pupils and particularly the attitude of individual teachers and heads.

31. Nearly all schools in the survey had prefects and head boys and/or girls. The average proportion of pupils per school who were intermediate or full prefects at any one time was about 10 per cent. Half the schools, especially those that were large or in urban areas, particularly in London, had school councils and just under half had prefects' councils and/or sixth-form societies (Appendix Tables A2.4 and A2.5).

32. A distinction has been made between the two-thirds of the schools in the survey whose prefects were a teacher-selected élite and the one-third of schools where all sixth-formers or comparatively large proportions of pupils became prefects.

33. In all schools with prefects, their responsibilities included supervision of other pupils and assistance to teachers. In a quarter of the schools, prefects' responsibilities also included involvement with welfare activities (Appendix Table A2.6).

34. There was little evidence of pupil involvement in school

policy-making, although opportunities appeared to exist in a majority of schools through school councils or prefects' councils for pupils to raise important matters.

35. Typical of small schools was that they were mainly rural and well-established as comprehensive schools; they tended to have a lower turnover of staff and to use a smaller proportion of their allowances for posts of responsibility for duties connected with pupil welfare and administration. They were not generally sub-divided for organizational purposes and their pupils were less likely to be interviewed individually by senior staff about choice of subjects and and careers, or on entry to the school.

36. Welsh schools in the survey were mainly rural and small, while schools in the south of England were mainly urban and large. However, not all the regional differences can be explained by the urban/rural or size factors. For instance, in Welsh schools heads generally had less freedom to make their own appointment of teachers, and senior staff were less often consulted about new appointments; allowances were not so commonly allocated to posts concerned with careers advice; teachers (and pupils) in Wales spent very much more time on school examination work; and pupils were timetabled for more lesson time. The *order* of differences in administrative practices between schools in the four regions was generally the same: south, north, midlands and Wales, differences being greatest between the south of England and Wales.

It must be stressed that school administration cannot be evaluated unless related to its effect on pupils. Administration is only a means to an end and it is possible that a 'badly administered' school can nevertheless provide excellent education for its pupils through other qualities manifested by its teachers.

This study indicates, however, that running a modern comprehensive school requires not only a professional approach to teaching from all staff, but also a professional approach from senior staff to administration. It is hard to avoid the conclusion that it is becoming essential for existing and aspiring heads of comprehensive schools to receive formal training, not only in the practice but also in the theory of administration.

# CHAPTER THREE

# The School Curriculum and Pupil Welfare

*by* T. S. ROBERTSON

THE LAST chapter covered the internal organization of the school, the functional importance of the various grouping systems, and the delegation of responsibility. Here, we shall be concerned with another aspect of organization—the timetable, and the way in which the pupils are allocated to separate teaching groups.

The curriculum of any school reflects the policies, priorities and intentions of its leaders, after they have been subjected to the restrictions of teacher supply, buildings, finance, time and the quality of the pupils. The printed timetable provides evidence of these policies and restrictions and enables the researcher to see how much school time a pupil spends on different kinds of activity. It also shows the extent to which pupils of different ability meet each other and how much time is spent with different teachers.

The various timetabling techniques used in the comprehensive school will be described here, together with the grouping of pupils: we then look in detail at the organization and special needs of pupils in the first three years, the fourth and fifth years and, lastly, in the sixth form. At the first stage, welfare and settling down are problems that need special consideration; at the second, careers guidance and choice of course is considered; at the third, or last stage, the courses available in the sixth and its special problems are discussed. The chapter ends with a description of the deployment of staff and with the library provision in the schools.

In the present study 46 timetables were examined in detail and 20 schools were visited. In the schools visited, interviews were conducted, following loosely-structured schedules, with members of staff responsible for timetable construction, for sixth forms, careers guidance, counselling, settling down in school and for library provision. The purpose of the interviews was to confirm or elucidate matters already examined in the timetables and other papers received from the schools.

The schools studied varied enormously on every conceivable criterion. It is impossible to think, therefore, in terms of 'typical comprehensive schools'; one can only record the variety and try to relate the variations in timetable and curriculum to the organization of the schools and their policies. The size and origin of the schools are the two dimensions which seem to have the greatest influence on the timetable and curriculum; size because of the limitations it imposes or freedom it provides, origin, through its relationship to the ability of the pupil intake and the traditions and policies of the school and its staff.

## Timetabling devices

The curriculum has two major dimensions: content and time. So firmly entrenched in the British secondary schooling system are the sub-divisions of these into 'subjects' and 'periods' respectively that it could hardly be expected that timetables would use any other units. The sub-division of school pupil populations has been discussed by Yates (1966), in *Grouping in Education*. Grouping by age is almost universal in British schools, and grouping by ability is nearly as fundamental in secondary education. The coinage or 'currency' of timetabling is therefore three-dimensional: each unit has a content dimension (subject), a time dimension (period) and a pupil grouping dimension (class or form).

In the construction of a timetable each unit has to be placed in a particular location (such as a classroom, laboratory or playing-field) and almost invariably in the charge of one member of staff. The arrangement of these three-dimensional units is considered in this chapter. Other aspects, such as teaching methods and materials, although they undoubtedly contribute to the effectiveness of education, were not studied. What will be considered are the arrangements of the units and how they contribute towards the aims of comprehensive education and, in particular, whether the doors of educational opportunity at the later stages remain open so far as is possible to pupils of all abilities.

Chapter 2, examining administration and communication in 50 schools, found 20 different ways of arranging the basic working week. Periods varied both in number and length. In our study of the curriculum and timetable it was found that variations on these two dimensions reflect two opposing trends:

(a) the replication of larger numbers of sometimes shorter periods, in order to meet the many demands for time in the curriculum;

(b) the reduction in the number of periods with consequent

increase in their length, to reduce time lost and disturbance between lessons, particularly where movement between buildings is involved.

Arrangements used to increase the number of periods available include the operation of two-week and six-day timetables. Devices used to reduce the number of periods include the four-period day, divided only by the lunch-hour and by mid-morning and afternoon breaks, and the allocation of larger teaching blocks to particular activities. The latter, unlike the former, does not generally extend through the whole timetable.

A common timetabling arrangement places certain classes, usually of the same age-group, simultaneously in blocks wherever they appear in the week. In one variation of this, all classes in a block will be studying the same subject at the same time; this allows 'setting' by ability in that subject to differ from the class grouping adopted for other subjects. Another timetabling variation involves several different subjects being timetabled simultaneously, so that the pupil can make a choice of subject in that 'option-block'. This enables the total range of subjects to be extended, without necessarily increasing the number of subjects each pupil studies. This opting for one subject rather than another usually marks a step towards specialization and commitment, since the choice of one of a group of subjects implies rejection of others. Complete rejection is avoided if a subject appears in more than one option-block. A further variation of the use of option-blocks is the differentiation into major and minor subjects.

Setting is common for the teaching of academic subjects, particularly English, French and Mathematics, but it is not confined to them. Option-blocks, on the other hand, are more often found for practical subjects, although they do often operate for academic subjects in the middle and later years of secondary schooling. The occurence of both setting and option-blocks in the schools of this study will be examined at each of the three stages—first to third years; fourth to fifth years; and sixth forms.

### The first to third years

*Placing Pupils in Teaching Groups on Entry*

A recent NFER report (1969) showed that, as local education authorities adopt systems of comprehensive secondary education, they are turning away from measuring the ability and attainment of pupils. If, however, as will be shown, practically every school adopts some system of ability grouping, the onus of allocation and the need to adjust the initial allocation where necessary after a settling-down period, falls on the school.

Few schools drew their intakes from a definite number of primary schools in any simple way. The rural schools with two- or three-form entry tended to receive their pupils from 10 or more village schools, and in some cases a child might be the only entrant from his junior school. The schools in towns which serve surrounding rural areas were usually fed principally by two or three urban primary and also a large number (from eight to 20) of village schools. The schools in dense urban areas also drew largely from several neighbouring schools, but also from many other more distant ones, each contributing from one to six pupils. It is, therefore, hardly surprising that allocation to teaching groups was fairly imprecise, resulting in the great overlap of ability in streams, bands and sets to be shown in later pages of this report.

In most cases, the attainment and assessment information formerly used by local education authorities is now available to heads of the secondary schools. This information includes the results of standardized tests of verbal reasoning, primary school records, pupil profiles and primary heads' recommendations. In some schools every child was interviewed before or after acceptance. There appeared to be three schools of thought on allocation; (a) an initial allocation with only a minor adjustment later; (b) an initial provisional allocation with major re-shuffling in the first few weeks or months in the secondary school, and (c) the deliberate mixing of abilities on entry followed by gradual separation over the following two or three years based on first-hand knowledge of the pupil. The last of these was infrequent in the schools visited; the other two occurred with approximately equal frequency. The comprehensive school project will include a study of pupil movements between ability groups as they pass through the schools; this will be reported in a later publication. From this special study it will be possible to assess the flexibility of the various grouping and setting systems.

## The Ability and Social Class of the Pupils

The wide variety of intakes to different comprehensive schools, in terms of pupils' intellectual ability and social class, has been described in the earlier report (Monks, 1968). Chapter 4 of this publication amplifies and confirms the general findings of the first survey, but in this case the information on attainment is based on test score results and not on estimates of school performance. The pupils included in the attainment survey sat three tests—English, arithmetic and non-verbal ability (the NF68). Whereas in Chapter 4 the ability of the intake of the whole school is considered, here we are looking at the ability of the pupils in the various forms of the intake.

In one school the intake of 111 pupils was unstreamed, and there was no setting of pupils in ability groups for any subject. The distribution of ability of pupils in the intake is represented in Diagram 3.1.

DIAGRAM 3.1: *The distribution of ability in intake (School 209)*

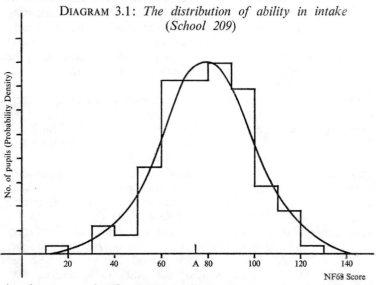

A=the mean value for 8,074 pupils in 45 comprehensive schools.

The smooth curve is superimposed on the percentage frequency histogram (111 pupils) from which it was derived. The histograms have been omitted from subsequent diagrams in this chapter.

In a second school the pupils in the first year were unstreamed, but placed in three sets for French, with a fourth 'non-language' set taking a technical subject. The overall distribution of ability of the first-year pupils was, as might be expected, similar to that of the preceding school. The smoothed distribution of scores for the pupils in each of the three French sets and the technical set is shown in Diagram 3.2.

Although the average scores of each of the four sets show a regular decrease with set number there is, as might be expected, considerable

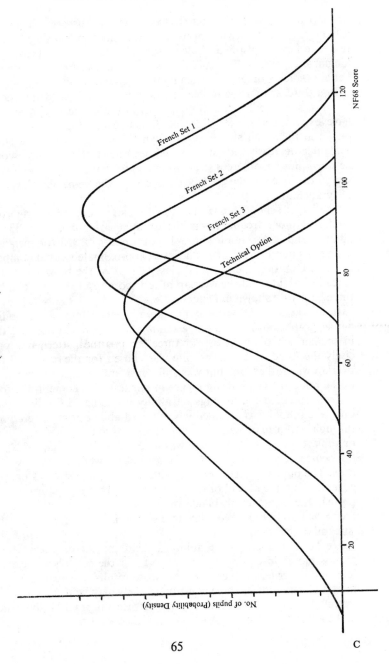

DIAGRAM 3.2: *The distribution of ability in four sets of first-year pupils*
*(School 029)*

French Set 1

French Set 2

French Set 3

Technical Option

NF68 Score

No. of pupils (Probability Density)

overlap in the scores of pupils from the various sets. If general attainment and ability are of minor significance in learning French, this overlap is justified, indeed special aptitude for learning a language together with general or specific motivation may prove a better predictor of language facility than general ability.

In a third school the intake of 285 pupils was divided into seven streams, supposedly on ability. In this instance one might perhaps have expected a clearer differentiation between the test scores of pupils in the seven streams. Although the average scores do show a regular decrease with stream number, the overlap in test scores between those in different streams remains considerable—pupils with scores of 70 could be in any class except the remedial class (see Diagram 3.3).

The larger schools tended not to adopt streaming of this rigorous kind and more frequent was the grouping of pupils into 'broad ability bands'. A school with a 12-form entry of 353 for instance, divided its pupils into three bands with approximately equal numbers in each. Omitting the remedial class (a part of the third band) the spread of ability and the overlap of test score results of those in the three bands are shown in Diagram 3.4.

In all the schools where pupils were grouped into broad ability bands, graphs of the same shape and relationship were obtained, and in smaller schools with two or three streams the pattern was precisely the same. If a smaller élite was chosen for the top band the overlap was rather less, but was still considerable, with some pupils in the bottom band scoring higher in our test than some in the top.

To summarize the findings on ability grouping in the first year, only one school was included where mixed-ability groups were used throughout. In all others, streaming or ability grouping in either bands or subject sets was used. There was a considerable overlap of NF68 test scores between pupils in different groups, whatever system was used. The pupils in small schools with two or three streams had, in general, the same spread of test scores when grouped by form as did those in the 'broad ability bands' of the large schools. In other words, the 'broad ability band' of the large school is no different from the 'stream' of the small school.

We hope to look at the ability and attainment of streams and groups more closely in the next report, for the schools are clearly selecting on criteria other than test score results. A break-down of the NF68 test into its three constituent parts may help shed light on the relative importance of the two subjects Reading and Mathematics in the selection procedure.

DIAGRAM 3.3: *The distribution of ability of first-year pupils in seven streams (School 253)*

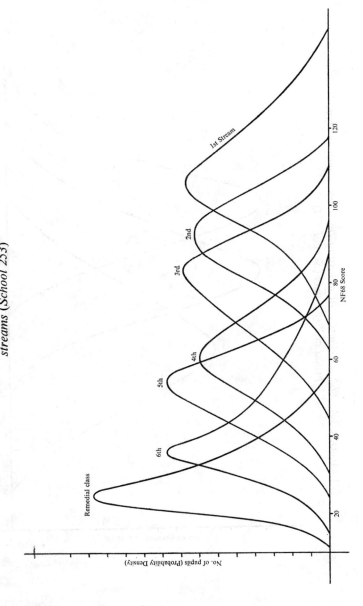

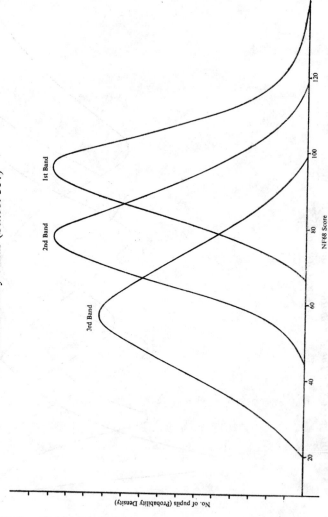

DIAGRAM 3.4: *The distribution of ability of first-year pupils in three broad ability bands (School 314)*

The fact that boys and girls from the more favourable homes are more frequently found in the upper streams, no doubt explains, at least in some measure, the overlap of test scores. In schools where detailed information of parental occupation was available, the relationship between ability group and social class (based on father's occupation) was studied. All social classes were represented in each stream or band. However, there was usually, although not invariably, a significantly greater proportion of pupils with parents in higher social class occupations in the upper than the lower bands or streams. This is in accord with the findings of other surveys such as those by Barker Lunn (1970), Douglas (1964) and Himmelweit (1966).

Diagram 3.5 gives the proportion of pupils in each social class in one school which grouped its first-year pupils into two broad bands of ability. Pupils in social classes I and II were roughly twice as likely to be in the upper band as those from classes IV and V.

DIAGRAM 3.5: *Percentages of first-year pupils with fathers in different occupations (School 063)*

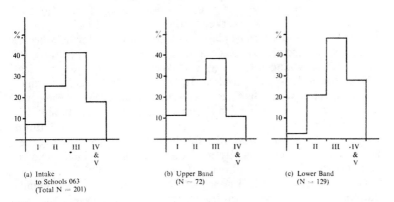

(a) Intake
to Schools 063
(Total N = 201)

(b) Upper Band
(N = 72)

(c) Lower Band
(N = 129)

In most schools this same social class pattern associated with streaming or banding was found, although in a few cases the trend, mainly because of the small number of pupils with fathers in non-manual occupations, was not sufficiently large to be statistically significant.

It is interesting to note that in the French ability groups of the otherwise unstreamed school already referred to in Diagram 3.2,

69

there were no significant social class differences between the groups, but perhaps this is not surprising, for the overlap of ability between the sets was considerable and more than that noted for schools grouping their pupils for more subjects.

## Pupil Welfare and Settling Down

Generally speaking, when a child moves from primary to secondary school he ceases to be in the charge of one teacher for virtually the whole of the school day and finds himself with a succession of different subject teachers. The move is also usually from a smaller to a larger school. Consequently, some pupils may have difficulty in becoming orientated to their new surroundings and settling down. It is important that one teacher should have primary responsibility for the welfare of each pupil, and it is usually convenient to combine this responsibility with registration and other related administrative duties. Traditionally, the form teacher has had these responsibilities, and in most of the schools visited this was still so. A disadvantage of this system is that the form teacher, usually a subject teacher, probably teaches his own form for only a small part of the week or possibly not even at all; this gives him little personal knowledge of the pupils. Also there is a marked tendency (Monks, 1968) for young, inexperienced teachers to be placed in charge of junior forms, when in fact pupil welfare needs considerable experience. A rapid turnover of many of the younger teachers, particularly in some geographical areas, also adds to this problem. It is notable that in all the small schools visited which had relatively stable staffing, the heads had chosen experienced teachers to take the first forms. Often this responsibility for welfare was not defined but assumed as a natural part of the teacher's work. In the large schools, however, other arrangements were frequently made, and a clearly defined chain of responsibility for pupil welfare usually existed.

Of the 20 schools visited none had purpose-built house accommodation, but systems based on house, school and years were encountered. In several instances, there was a head of lower school who acted virtually as the headmaster of the smaller unit, allocating responsibility for welfare to year masters, form teachers or tutors. In this way the advantages of the 'small school' were regained—the head and some member of his staff knowing every pupil individually. In other cases pupils were placed under the care of tutors who had a stated responsibility to get to know each child and to act as a counsellor. Some tutors were responsible for a vertical group of pupils spanning all ages, with the older pupils sharing some responsibility for the younger. In other cases the tutor had a horizontal group all the same age, and moved up through the school with them. Since the tutor probably did not teach all his pupils it was generally thought necessary for schools adopting this system to timetable some special tutorial periods.

When the intake is divided by a method other than streaming, it is possible to form the primary groups according to other criteria, such as mixed-ability forms, and forms within broad ability bands. Attempts to assist settling in by placing pupils from the same village in the same form, or pupils from the same primary school together, were often used, but not always successfully. In one case the head said:

> 'In past years we put all children from the same school in the same class. They settled down too well, creating disciplinary problems because of over-confidence.'

Another head distributed children from primary schools to different classes but ensured that every child knew at least one child in his class.

An example of a clearly-defined settling-in procedure was described as follows:

> 'The method of selection helps us to know the pupil and the parent. Because of over-subscription the entry is selective. Selection is based on: (a) a report from the primary school (Junior School Profile); and (b) an interview of every prospective pupil with his parents, by the head, deputy head and head of lower school.
>
> 'Parents of pupils accepted are invited to a meeting (in the summer term) to find out about the school. They bring their children to the school on the first day, when they meet the head of lower school, the year teacher and the form teacher. A conscious effort is then made at all levels to know the children as soon as possible. During the first term there are continuing contacts and discussions involving form teachers, children, remedial teachers, year teachers, head of lower school, welfare and care agencies, primary heads (desirable over problems of adjustment) and parents. A general report is made to parents at the end of the first term, not a 'subject report' but a progress report with emphasis on how well the child is settling in. Arising out of the report a general meeting for first-year parents follows, early in the spring term, where form teachers see parents individually.'

Many heads mentioned the advantages of having specific individual members of staff who, by their personal qualities and perhaps experience, were able to take on responsibility for the welfare of younger pupils and assist them in settling in. Often the qualities of individuals were considered more important than defined systems of responsibility, and more than one head said that the effectiveness of the defined system varied according to the personal qualities of the teachers.

## The Curriculum in the First Three Years

Typically, there was some distinction, right from the start of secondary schooling, between the curricula of the more and less able pupils. The more able tended to take a foreign language (or an extra foreign language) and the less able to spend more time on practical subjects. However, the differences were usually small, and a typical subject break-down is shown in Table 3.1.

TABLE 3.1: *Curriculum in the first year in one school* (*School 253*)

|  | NO. OF PERIODS | | |
|---|---|---|---|
|  | *Upper Stream* | *Lower Stream* | *Remedial Class* |
| English .. .. .. | 6 | 9 | 11 |
| Maths. .. .. .. | 6 | 8 | 7 |
| History .. .. .. | 3 | 2 | 2 |
| Geography .. .. | 3 | 3 | 2 |
| French .. .. .. | 5 | — | — |
| Science .. .. .. | 4 | 2 | 2 |
| Art, Craft, Handicraft | 4 | 7 | 7 |
| Music, RE, PE, Games | 9 | 9 | 9 |
| *Total* .. .. .. | 40 | 40 | 40 |

Many of the 46 schools taught French to all first-year classes except the remedial class. This common curriculum means that no pupils in lower classes are barred by their lack of knowledge from the possibility of moving upstream. With modern methods of language tuition (using an oral approach) the learning of a foreign language need not be an academic burden for the less able pupils.

In the second and third years the divergence increased between a more academic timetable for the upper groups and a more practical one for the lower groups. In some schools the better linguists were introduced to Latin or a second foreign language—the larger schools offered a choice of Spanish, German and Russian. The upper bands or streams tended to take three science subjects, while the lower bands tended to take only a general science or rural science course.

Where there were varied facilities for practical subjects pupils were often introduced to a range and then opted for some rather than others. For instance, in the first year all pupils might take music, art and woodwork or housecraft but, later, the range of practical subjects increases, academic pupils taking a smaller selection and non-academic pupils a larger. In some mixed schools the traditional division into boys' and girls' practical subjects was discarded, and some boys took housecraft and some girls technical subjects. A typical range of practical subjects available in a larger school comprised woodwork, metalwork, technical drawing, needlework, housecraft, art and craft (including pottery). Music, art and drama also appeared with these in option blocks in some schools.

## The Onset of Specialization

The selection of an additional foreign language or practical subject is perhaps a first step towards specialization, but it is usually not until the fourth year that specialization may be said to begin. It is during the third year that staff and pupils make decisions which will become effective in the fourth. Although in most schools pupils in the lower groups, theoretically, have the opportunity of continuing an academic course leading to GCE or CSE qualifications, it is suspected that such cases are very few, at least in some schools; in practice allocation to a lower stream or band may restrict, at an early age, the pupil's later course and future career. The Foundation's follow-up of pupils in the later stages at school and the changes between streams should provide evidence to confirm or refute this.

All schools visited had systems of consultation between subject teachers, heads of departments, pupils, parents and the head. The final decision on any controversial choice by a pupil lay sometimes with the head and sometimes with the parent. A typical sequence for consultation, as described by a head in interview, was as follows:

'At Easter there is a third-year examination. The staff set this to determine the pupil's gift for a subject. There are then consultations between the pupil and his tutor group leader, followed by staff meetings to discuss the pupil's examination results, attitude and his wishes as expressed to his tutor. At these meetings loose recommendations are reached. Juggling to make up the numbers in the teaching groups then takes place. A letter is then sent to parents, explaining the courses and the school's recommendations for the individual pupil. They are invited to come and discuss these if they wish. The last word is always with the parent, but influence is brought to bear.'

Since choice of subjects is closely linked to intended career, the careers advisory staff were sometimes brought into the consultation at this stage. One careers master said:

> 'Starting in the Spring term of the third year the careers officer from the Youth Employment Bureau gives the third-year pupils a general talk. This is followed by a Careers Convention. Pupils then make options for their fourth-year subjects.'

A summary of the provision for careers guidance, of which the selection of fourth-form careers is a part, will be briefly described later in this chapter.

### The fourth and fifth years

*Ability Grouping and Social Class*

With few exceptions, it was on transfer from the third to the fourth year that major changes in the spread of subjects, accompanied by re-grouping of pupils, occurred. Although several schools had mixed ability groups for some subjects, no school in this sub-sample used mixed ability groups throughout the middle years of secondary schooling. The main ways in which pupils were grouped in the fourth year can be summarized as:

1. streaming and banding on ability;
2. setting on ability in separate subjects;
3. choices of subjects from option blocks;
4. division into leavers and non-leavers;
5. division into courses of a vocational nature;
6. various combinations of these.

A distinction between prospective 'O' level, CSE and non-examination candidates was often made, either firmly or tentatively and an additional classification, of those pupils sitting 'O' level a year early, whether in all or a few selected subjects, was sometimes made. Several schools had a policy of entering every pupil for an external examination—GCE, CSE or another of a less exacting standard.

Corresponding to the study of the ability of the first-years and their grouping into streams or bands is a study of the fourth-years. Diagram 3.6 gives an example of the spread of ability in each of three streams in one school. When pupils were divided into vocational courses there were usually also differences of ability between the various groups. An example of this is shown in Table 3.2. The table shows that the 95 pupils on academic courses were clearly separated from the remainder. With the exception of those doing building, however, differences between the other groups were slight.

DIAGRAM 3.6: *The distribution of ability of fourth-year pupils in three streams (School 192)*

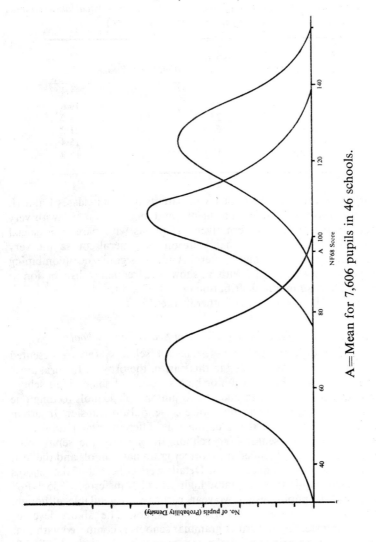

A = Mean for 7,606 pupils in 46 schools.

Social class is closely related to choice of course at this stage. This is shown, using data from another school, in Table A3.2 and Diagram 3.7. The spread of pupils from each social class in each course was

TABLE 3.2 *Mean scores of pupils doing various vocational courses in the fourth year (School 127)*

| COURSE | NO. OF PUPILS | NF68 MEAN SCORE | SD |
|---|---|---|---|
| Academic .. .. | 95 | 130·9 | 11·8 |
| Commercial .. | 41 | 99·5 | 19·8 |
| Design .. .. | 22 | 99·0 | 18·9 |
| Engineering .. | 65 | 96·9 | 21·2 |
| General .. .. | 21 | 92·8 | 15·4 |
| Building .. .. | 18 | 78·3 | 16·9 |

large. However, of the pupils with parents in social classes I and II, almost two-thirds were on academic and modern courses, with very few on the general. Alternatively, of pupils with parents in social classes IV and V, almost half were on the general course and very few on the academic and modern. A test of significance (combining classes I with II, and IV with V) shows the frequency distribution to differ from a random distribution ($\chi^2 = 19·22$, d.f.$=4$, $p < 0·01$). This is in line with the findings of other workers.

### The Operation of a System of Choice of Senior High School

Several different two-tier systems of schools were represented among the schools included in this part of the project. In rural areas the relationship between junior high school and senior high school was usually simple, with one or two junior high schools feeding one senior, so that there was no choice of school on transfer. In urban and suburban areas, the situation was different, and pupils often had a choice of senior high school. In one city the senior high schools could be classified into former grammar schools and the rest. These schools had equal status. Details were collected of the schools to which pupils from a junior high school transferred. The NF68 scores of the pupils, tested two years earlier, were available, although, unfortunately, parental occupation was not. The ability level of pupils transferring to former grammar schools is compared with that of those transferring to former non-grammar schools in Table 3.3.

DIAGRAM 3.7: *Percentages of fourth-year pupils with fathers in different occupations (School 028)*

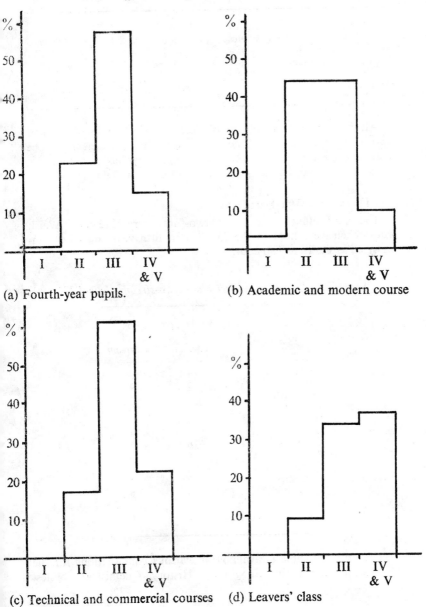

(a) Fourth-year pupils.

(b) Academic and modern course

(c) Technical and commercial courses

(d) Leavers' class

TABLE 3.3: *Mean scores of pupils transferring to senior high schools two years later (School 253)*

| PUPILS TRANSFERRING TO FORMER— | NO. OF PUPILS | NF68 MEAN SCORE | SD | RANGE |
|---|---|---|---|---|
| Non-Grammar Schools | 78 | 61·9 | 25·5 | 22–124 |
| Grammar Schools | 89 | 81·9 | 18·6 | 21–135 |

Although both types of school were receiving pupils of a broad spread of ability from this one junior high school, it is clear that the former grammar schools received very highly significantly more able pupils than the former non-grammar schools ($p < 0.001$).

### The Fourth- and Fifth-Year Curriculum

The curriculum of a small two-form-entry streamed Welsh comprehensive school in the fourth and fifth years may be summarized as shown in Table 3.4.

TABLE 3.4: *Fourth-year curriculum (two-stream. School 371)*

| | NO. OF PERIODS | |
|---|---|---|
| | A Stream | B Stream |
| Welsh | 4 | 4 |
| English | 5 | 5 |
| Mathematics | 6 | 3 |
| Option I | 5 | 0 |
| Option II | 6 | 6 |
| Option III | 6 | 4 |
| Option IV | 6 | 6 |
| Practical Subs. | 4 | 8 |
| Current Affairs | 0 | 2 |
| Gen. Science | 0 | 4 |
| Games and PE | 6 | 6 |
| *Total* | 48 | 48 |

The optional subjects available in various combinations for the A stream were Latin, Geography, History, Chemistry, Physics,

Scripture, French, Music, Agricultural Science and Biology. For the B stream, the only options were Geography/History and Music/Agricultural Science with Typing available as an extra. The subjects collectively described above as 'practical subjects', were Art, Housecraft, Needlework and Woodwork.

By comparison, Table 3.5 shows the curriculum for the fourth-years of a large urban comprehensive school dividing its fourth form into three broad bands of ability.

TABLE 3.5: *Fourth-year curriculum (large urban. School 273)*

|  | NO. OF PERIODS | |
| --- | :---: | :---: |
|  | A and B Bands | C Band |
| English (setted) .. .. | 6 | 6 |
| Mathematics (setted) .. | 5 | 5 |
| Option I .. .. .. | 4 | 3 |
| Option II .. .. .. | 4 | 3 |
| Option III .. .. .. | 4 | 3 |
| Option IV .. .. .. | 4 | 3 |
| Option V .. .. .. | 2 | 4 |
| PE and Games .. .. | 3 | 4 |
| Modern Language .. .. | 0 | 1 |
| Music, RI and Form Period.. | 3 | 3 |
| *Total* .. .. .. | 35 | 35 |

The option blocks were varied from year to year to meet as closely as possible the choices of the pupils. In 1967/68, they were as in Table 3.6.

The advantage of two sets, one working for 'O' level and the other for CSE, was that in the upper set traditional academic content and methods could be used, whereas in the lower there could be greater freedom for the teacher to choose the content and methods to suit the pupils' capabilities. Since Grade 1 in CSE is generally accepted as equivalent to 'O' level, allocation to Set 2 did not close the door to an academic career. Pupils placed in the bottom band were, however, virtually excluded from an academic career, although in this particular school there was a well-defined method of consultation between pupil, parents and staff before entry to the fourth form: in the case of disagreement between school and parents, the final choice lay with

TABLE 3.6: *Subject options for fourth-years in a large urban school (School 273)*

| OPTIONS: | I | II | III | IV | V |
|---|---|---|---|---|---|
| A & B Bands | French (1)† GCE<br>French (2) CSE<br>Tech. Drawing (1)<br>Tech. Drawing (2)<br>Geog. (1) GCE<br>Geog. (2) CSE<br>Dom. Sci. (1)<br>Dom. Sci. (2)<br>Dom. Sci. (3)<br>Rural Science<br>Music | French<br>Metalwork<br>History (1) GCE<br>History (2) CSE<br>German<br>Spanish<br>Biology (1)<br>Biology (2)<br>Typing (1) CSE<br>Typing (2) CSE | Geography<br>Art<br>Latin<br>Chemistry (1) GCE<br>Chemistry (2) CSE<br>Biology<br>Commerce (1) CSE<br>Commerce (2) CSE<br>Woodwork | History (1)<br>History (2)<br>Tech. Drawing CSE<br>RI<br>Geography<br>French (1) GCE<br>French (2) CSE<br>Physics (1) GCE<br>Physics (2) CSE<br>Art (1)<br>Art (2) | Art (1)<br>Art (2)<br>Pottery<br>Metalwork (1)<br>Metalwork (2)<br>Woodwork (1)<br>Woodwork (2)<br>Dom. Sci. (1)<br>Dom. Sci. (2)<br>Needlework (1)<br>Needlework (2)<br>Drama |
| C Band | Art<br>Needlework<br>Needlework<br>B. Tech. | Motor Mech.<br>Metalwork<br>Family Care<br>Hist./Geog. | Art<br>Leisure Studies<br>Tech. Drawing<br>Typing | Dom. Sci.<br>Dom. Sci.<br>Science<br>Rural Science | Modern Society<br>(4 periods)<br>or Gen. Course<br>(Careers<br>Social & Local<br>History<br>International<br>Affairs). |

† Numbers in brackets indicate ability sets.

the parent. Furthermore, allocation to the bottom band did not exclude a pupil from entry to the sixth form, for there was no academic barrier in this school and any pupil who completed his previous course satisfactorily might enter the sixth.

To see how basic and optional subjects were timetabled across the eight forms in this school, it is sufficient to look at one seven-period day, shown in Table 3.7. The 240 pupils were in their own forms for one period only (Period 5). At other times they were divided into 10 ability sets for English and Mathematics or 14 or 15 option groups.

The operation of this setting system involved five members of the English staff and five of the mathematics staff simultaneously, and this restriction must have reduced the freedom of the timetabler to manoeuvre the units elsewhere in the timetable. There was a disadvantage with the option-groups containing practical and academic subjects, for the former might be better taught in longer teaching periods than the latter. Although the forms were said to comprise a broad band of ability, it is clear that the C Band spent no time (at least not on the day in question) with pupils from other Bands. Although the A and B Bands shared option-groups, there was setting within the option-groups, and probably some options (such as rural science and metalwork) attracted few able pupils. The mixing of pupils by ability was therefore probably not marked, even in the A and B Bands. These are the disadvantages (at least as far as the comprehensive principle is involved) and they must be set against the advantages referred to earlier.

Although in this school there was no system of courses (such as academic, technical, or commercial), it is clear that pupils, particularly in the A and B Bands, could select options which provided fairly specialized courses; alternatively, their choices could be broad and unspecialized.

In another school with a somewhat similar option block system, a member of staff had calculated that there were 2,250 theoretical subject combinations. If certain subjects such as Metalwork, were selected only by boys, and others such as Needlework only by girls, the number of possible combinations was reduced to 510 for each sex. Since there were only 220 pupils, each could have had a different selection. In fact, the 220 pupils selected 124 distinct combinations of optional subjects, no one combination being chosen by more than 14 pupils.

When such a wide choice is available, it is essential that pupils should receive sound educational advice, and nearly all schools visited had defined systems of consultation between pupils, parents,

TABLE 3.7: *One day in the fourth-form timetable of a comprehensive school (School 273)*

| Forms (in three broad ability bands) | 1 | 2 | 3 and 4 | 5 | 6 and 7 |
|---|---|---|---|---|---|
| | | Option II | Option I | | Option IV |
| 4Ai | English (5 sets) | French | French (2 sets) | RE | History (2 sets) |
| 4Aii | | Metalwork | Tech. Drawing (2 sets) | Music | Tech. Drawing |
| 4Aiii | | History (2 sets) | Geography (2 sets) | PE | RE |
| 4Bi | | German | Domestic Science (3 sets) | | Geography |
| | | Spanish | Rural Science | PE | French (2 sets) |
| 4Bii | Mathematics (5 sets) | Biology (2 sets) | Music | RE | Physics (2 sets) |
| 4Biii | | Typing (2 sets) | | Music | Art (2 sets) |
| 4Ci | | Motor Mechanics | Art | French or German | Domestic Science (2 sets) |
| 4Cii | | Metalwork | Needlework | | Science |
| | | Family Care | Building Technology | | Rural Science |
| | | History and Geography | | | |

PERIODS

class teachers, heads of departments, heads and their deputies. An example of one of these systems was described earlier (page 273). At any point where important decisions (such as choice of optional subjects, staying on or leaving school, entering the sixth form) had to be made, consultation procedures existed. Often compromises would have to be made; for example, a pupil's ability in a subject might not be such that the subject teacher would recommend him to continue with it, even if the pupil felt he needed it for his intended career. Ideally, careers advice should be available from the age at which pupils are required to opt for some subjects rather than others, but, in many cases, does not become available until after this, when the pupil is in the fourth year, perhaps having already decided to leave at 15. It seems therefore appropriate to consider careers guidance under the general heading of 'the fourth and fifth years at school'.

*Careers Guidance*

In grammar schools, careers guidance is largely orientated towards the professions and, in particular, is much concerned with college and university entrance. In secondary modern schools, it is orientated rather towards non-professional employment and apprenticeships. The comprehensive school has to cater not only for the education of a broad range of pupils but also for careers guidance and counselling. The careers guidance procedures in 19 schools were studied, and it was found that there were about as many systems as there were schools. This reflected the variety of the schools, and the differences of local career prospects. The big division in prospects lay between the urban and rural schools. Generally speaking, in the Inner London Education Authority area and most urban schools, prospects were good, particularly if pupils were willing to travel. At the opposite extreme, however, were the English and Welsh rural schools where, except for unskilled work, pupils staying on at school and entering further education were more or less obliged to move out of the area.

In one small school the head was in charge of careers guidance, and in two others (a very large school and a very small one) the deputy head was responsible. In some schools there was a head of the careers department, but more frequently a subject teacher had the additional responsibility for careers. Some of these teachers were also heads of their own subject departments, and it is perhaps worth noting that one head volunteered the information that the master responsible for careers was so busy with his own department that he had little time to spend on careers advice. It would be wrong, however, to suggest that careers advice was available from one source only, for many members of staff with special knowledge of various fields of employment, e.g. technical and commercial staff, and those with special knowledge of the pupils, e.g. house masters and mistresses, were often involved.

In those schools where sixth-form pupils were aiming at university and college entrance, the responsibility for advice fell outside the scope of the careers master or mistress, generally on to a member of staff in charge of a sixth form.

For those not staying at school and aiming at higher education, careers guidance and information was offered and given by a number of people and agencies. The Youth Employment Service was named by all schools, and formed a regular part of the guidance offered. Three schools also named the Careers Advisory Service. Timetabled periods for careers were a feature of most schools, but these were often only for fourth-year leavers and not for those staying on at school, with equally important subject decisions to make which might well shape their courses of study in the sixth form and later. Careers conventions were frequently mentioned, but whereas these were comparatively easy to organize in the urban schools, they were much more difficult in remote rural areas. Regular weekly careers afternoons for leavers' classes were organized in some schools. In these the careers staff arranged a programme of discussions by various speakers, conventions and industrial visits. The success of these was enhanced if preliminary 'briefings' were held, and pupils were given a series of tasks to perform and report upon in connection with each visit.

The physical facilities available to the careers departments varied enormously. For example, one careers department had as its only facility a notice and display board at the entrance to the library. Another had a very well-provided careers annexe, where the careers teacher spent every lunch hour and was available to talk informally to any pupil who wished. Here careers publications and pamphlets were available for pupils to consult at leisure. In most schools, however, the careers teacher had to use his locker, sometimes supplemented by a filing cabinet, but essentially storing all careers literature under lock and key.

The general impressions gained on talking with the members of staff involved, and asking what were the advantages and shortcomings of the advice they were able to offer, were as follows:

84

1. the former grammar schools can learn much from the experience acquired in the former secondary modern schools;

2. the advice available to 'early leavers' is often more comprehensive than that available to pupils leaving at the end of the fifth year. If a gap exists, it is in the advice given to pupils who are neither in the fourth-year leavers' classes nor in the academic group staying on into the sixth;

3. the quality of the advice given reflects the enthusiasm and personal qualities of the careers staff. These, in turn, can be fostered by recognition, in terms of status, salary and career prospects, the time allocated on the timetable, and the physical facilities available. The latter includes storage and display space, and information rooms. A careers teacher needs to have time to plan and organize a course, and needs to spend a fair amount of time speaking to his pupils, if necessary outside teaching hours;

4. careers advice needs to be linked, as it is in some schools, to other advice, particularly as to choice of subjects, as early as this arises—usually in the third form.

## The sixth form

### Sizes of Sixth Forms

In the first report (Monks, 1968), a brief look was taken at the size of sixth forms in comprehensive schools, including many whose pupils were not derived from a comprehensive intake. It was found that schools with 600 pupils or fewer had an average of 40 pupils in the sixth form, those with between 600 and 1,000 pupils an average of 60 and those with over 1,000 pupils an average of 110. Factors tending to give rise to small sixth forms included:

(a) the time taken to build up a sixth form in new schools or those recently designated comprehensive;

(b) dispersed rural catchment areas, giving rise to small schools;

(c) competition with grammar and other selective schools for the more able pupils in the catchment area;

(d) artificial restriction of the catchment by language (Welsh-speaking) or religion (denominational schools);

(e) and possibly segregation of boys and girls in separate schools.

Much has been written about the size at which a sixth form becomes a viable unit, able to give an adequate choice of subjects to pupils and to use specialist staff economically. However, absolute figures of the numbers of pupils are irrelevant if little or nothing is known about their educational standards.

Traditionally, sixth-formers have usually been assumed to be studying for 'A' level GCE, but this is changing. It was already known from previous work on this project that many of the comprehensive sixth-form pupils were not studying for these advanced exams. It is now possible to classify the sixth forms as they were when the current study of comprehensive schools was undertaken, in terms of the academic calibre of the pupils and the policy of the school on admission to the sixth form. It is clear that, in addition to the list of factors contributing to the small sixth form, there was the artificial barrier of excluding from entry pupils who failed to achieve a certain minimum academic standard. In some schools, for example, four 'O' level passes acted as the necessary passport. The reasons for imposing restrictions varied and some appeared to have a good foundation. In a small school, for instance, it may be impracticable to provide both academic and non-academic staff for only a small number of sixth-form pupils.

The sixth forms studied can be classified into four groups.

1. Traditional academic sixth forms, with minumum entrance requirements imposed. These may be large sixth forms (150 in one school) or small—28 in a two-form entry rural Welsh school. These traditional sixths were found in former grammar schools recently designated comprehensive with no 'comprehensive intake' pupils having reached the sixth. They were also found in schools that had been comprehensive for many years, where school policy excluded non-academic pupils in the sixth form.

2. Traditional academic sixth forms, now starting to admit non-academic pupils and providing the necessary courses. These might be said to be 'building downwards'.

3. Truly comprehensive sixth forms with no academic barriers and catering for pupils of a wide range of ability.

4. Sixth forms being 'built upwards' from academically mediocre origins. These occurred, for example, in schools heavily 'creamed' by grammar schools, in former secondary modern schools which had recently been designated 'comprehensive', and in some schools in socially underprivileged areas.

The composition of the sixth form was looked at closely in eighteen schools. Four had sixth forms which were not undergoing much change ('stationary' in Table 3.8)—two of them were traditionally academic and two comprehensive. In six schools there had been academic sixth forms which were being extended 'downwards' to cater for less academic pupils, while in the remaining eight schools there were sixth forms which were being built 'upwards' from a nucleus of pupils, not usually of very high ability. The numbers of pupils and, the way in which they were distributed between the first and second and final years are shown in Table 3.8.

TABLE 3.8: *Average number of sixth-formers in 18 schools*

| STATE OF DEVELOPMENT OF SIXTH FORM | FIRST-YEAR | SECOND- AND THIRD-YEAR | ALL |
|---|---|---|---|
| Building 'downwards' (6 schools) .. .. .. | 42 | 32 | 74 |
| Stationary (4 schools) .. .. .. | 34 | 18 | 52 |
| Building 'upwards' (8 schools) .. .. .. | 54 | 19 | 73 |
| *Total* .. .. .. | 45 | 24 | 69 |

Although this was a small non-random sample, the average size of sixth forms in the 18 schools fell close to the average found for 181 schools in the first report (69 to 70 pupils). Moreover, the ratio of pupils in the first-year sixth to pupils in the second- and third-year sixths was almost identical. This suggests that the figures for the 18 schools are reasonably representative of the larger population, and that there were roughly twice as many pupils in first-year sixths as in second- and third-year sixths combined. In the academic sixths building 'downwards' the sixth forms contained a greater proportion of pupils in the second- and third-year sixths, while in the sixths building 'upwards' there were fewer in the second and third year. This undoubtedly reflects the number of pupils who were spending only one year in the sixth. The attributes of some of these pupils will be examined in this chapter, with illustrations taken from sixth forms of different types given.

The numbers of pupils and the types of sixth form they were in are shown in Table 3.9.

TABLE 3.9: *Pupils in four contrasting sixth forms*

| SCHOOL CODE | 361 | 248 | 273 | 147 |
|---|---|---|---|---|
| Description of Sixth Form | Small, Academic, Welsh | Large, Urban Academic, Building Downwards | Large, Urban, Comprehensive | Urban, Creamed, Building Upwards |
| 1st-Year Pupils .. | 11 | 72 | 91 | 69 |
| 2nd- and 3rd-Year Pupils .. .. | 17 | 90 | 35 | 36 |
| Total .. .. | 28 | 162† | 126 | 105 |

† One-third of these reach the sixth by an 'accelerated stream' and spend three years in the sixth form; the 'output' is therefore correspondingly smaller.

The numbers of first-year sixth pupils and the type of work they do are shown in Table 3.10.

TABLE 3.10: *Courses taken by first-year sixth pupils in four contrasting sixth forms*

| SCHOOL CODE | 361 | 248 | 273 | 147 |
|---|---|---|---|---|
| 'A' level in at Least 1 Subject .. | 11 | 66 | 49 | 19 |
| Commercial Course .. .. | — | — | 20 | 35 |
| Other Non 'A' level Work Only .. | — | 6 | 22 | 15 |
| Total .. .. .. .. | 11 | 72 | 91 | 69 |

The 'A' level subjects available are listed in Table 3.11.

## Comparisons of Sixth Forms

In comparing these four sixth forms, it can be seen that 11 'A' level subjects were available in the small sixth form in the Welsh school and 14 in the developing school. Teaching groups in both schools were very small in some subjects. In the Welsh school, first- and second-year sixths were combined so that teaching groups were of a more economical size. In this school, there was mostly 'A' level work. In the developing sixth, on the other hand, there was little 'A' level work. Whereas in the Welsh school there could be little chance of increasing the numbers in the sixth (except by a change of policy), there is little doubt that in the other school numbers would rise in the course of time to give a more economical use of staff and facilities and a wider choice of courses.

TABLE 3.11: *The 'A' level subjects available in four contrasting sixth forms*

| School Code: | 361 | 248 | 264 | 147 |
|---|---|---|---|---|
| *Subject* | | | | |
| English | † | † | † | † |
| French | † | † | † | † |
| Welsh | † | | | |
| Latin | | † | | |
| German | | † | † | |
| Russian | | † | | |
| Spanish | | | † | |
| Geography | † | † | † | † |
| History | † | | † | † |
| Economics | | † | † | |
| RI | | | † | † |
| Art | † | † | † | † |
| Music | † | | | † |
| Mathematics | † | † | † | † |
| Further Maths. | | † | † | † |
| Physics | † | † | † | † |
| Chemistry | † | † | † | † |
| Biology | † | † | † | |
| Botany | | | | † |
| Zoology | | | | † |
| Housecraft | | | | † |
| Tech. Drawing | | † | † | |
| Woodwork | | † | † | |
| Metalwork | | † | † | |
| *Total* | 11 | 16 | 17 | 14 |

In the large comprehensive school, 17 'A' level subjects were available compared with 16 offered in the sixth form of the large 'academic' school, but teaching groups in some subjects were small in both schools. In none of the schools was there much bridging of the arts/science division but, as will be mentioned later, the availability of minority-time subjects, at least in the large comprehensive school, ameliorated the situation. In the large 'academic' school, an 'A' level general studies paper was taken by most pupils, to broaden the sixth-form curriculum. Although, in this school there were as yet few non 'A' level candidates in the sixth form, in the large comprehensive school the non 'A' level candidates were nearly as numerous as the 'A' level pupils in the first-year sixth.

*Organizing the Work of the Sixth Form*

In nearly every school visited, the final details of the subjects available, and the combinations of subjects, were adjusted as far as possible to meet the requests of intending pupils entering the sixth forms. However, the demand must to a large extent be influenced by the pattern of previous sixth forms and by the staff and facilities available.

In the few schools where entry to the sixth form was restricted to 'academic' pupils, the problems of timetabling were those of the grammar school, and need not be studied here. It is in the schools with unrestricted entry to the sixth that problems peculiar to comprehensive schools were found. Many heads, usually those making greatest efforts to solve the problems, felt that they had not yet reached a completely satisfactory solution. The chief problems mentioned were:

1. providing courses suitable for pupils who wished to stay on, 'some with no hope of gaining any GCE or CSE qualifications', and some only under parental pressure for a paper qualification;

2. catering for pupils able to take perhaps one 'A' level subject and a range of 'O' level and CSE subjects;

3. catering for pupils who could aim at a few 'O' level and CSE subjects in the sixth-form, either repeating these or starting them from scratch;

4. avoiding undesirable social divisions (for example that between upper and lower sixth, between academic and general sixth, or between arts and science sixth);

5. providing opportunities for all pupils to accept responsibility;

6. avoiding a restrictive 'school' atmosphere, treating sixth-formers as young adults, when in the words of one responder, 'some are not yet ready for this'.

Schools with established sixth forms, just starting to admit 'unqualified' pupils, tended for the first few years to admit these to a separate class, where they usually followed timetables individually arranged. If there was sufficient demand for a particular subject or subjects, these were timetabled and run as GCE or CSE one-year classes, many pupils repeating the subject. Otherwise pupils might be taking repeat 'O' levels or CSE classes with the fifth form, for a full range or merely a few subjects. However, in schools with established sixths, which had a number of years in which to build up the non 'A' level work, less makeshift arrangements were evident. For girls, commercial courses with their own timetable were frequently organized, sometimes at two levels in the same school—a 'post "O" level' commercial course, and one of a lower standard. This is particularly appropriate in urban schools in large cities. In some rural schools, however, it is less appropriate. For boys, separate courses in engineering, building and commerce were sometimes found, alongside traditional academic courses.

In a few schools the option-block system provided the opportunity for pupils to select a group of subjects with a bias towards a particular career. If the option blocks were of major subjects (generally 'A' level standard), and minor subjects ('O' level, CSE, or non-examination) many of the requirements of a true comprehensive sixth form were met. Academic sixth-formers could select two or three 'A' levels and minor subjects of a contrasting nature (practical or cultural) to provide a balanced course, and the sharp division between arts and science was avoided. Technically-orientated sixth-formers could select two or three practical 'A' levels and also continue to study a language or art. Pupils lacking 'O' level or CSE subjects might select solely 'minor' courses, or minor courses and one major ('A' level) course.

The school must be large enough, and have a sufficiently well-balanced intake, to carry the staff and facilities to provide this type of sixth form. However, one school with a nine-form entry, 1.450 pupils, and a fair range of ability and social class operated this system; 126 pupils were in the sixth form and there were 75 members of staff. The option-block system operating, which varied from year to year to meet, as far as possible, the requests of the pupils, is shown for this school in Table 3.12.

Typical 'A' level selections were English, History, French; Pure Mathematics, Physics, Chemistry; Metalwork, Woodwork, Engineering Drawing; Pure Mathematics, French, Economics. One or two minority subjects might also be selected from the option block not

TABLE 3.12: *The option-block system of sixth-form subjects in comprehensive school 273*

| OPTION BLOCK: | I | II | III | IV |
|---|---|---|---|---|
| *Major Subjects* (8 Periods) | Pure Maths<br>German<br>Metalwork | Physics<br>English<br>Home Economics<br>Woodwork<br>Economics | Chemistry<br>History<br>Eng. Drawing<br>Spanish<br>English | Biology<br>Applied Maths<br>French<br>Art |
| *Minor Subjects* (4 Periods) | *(a)* Maths ('O' level)  *(b)* French<br>Public Affairs<br>Statistics<br>Technical Drawing | *(a)* English Lang.  *(b)* Physics<br>English Lit.<br>Greek Civilization | *(a)* Metalwork for Scientists  *(b)* Geog.<br>Economics<br>Chem. | *(a)* Surveying  *(b)* Maths for Scientists<br>Chemistry  Biology |

*Note:* Commercial subjects are provided as a separate course.

already taken up by an 'A' level subject. A non 'A' level course might include subjects taken only from 'minor' options, for example, Mathematics, French, English Language, Geography, Biology. A mixed 'A' and 'O' level course might be 'A' level Art, with 'O' level Public Affairs, English Literature, Geography and Biology.

## Responsibilities and Privileges in the Sixth Form

The amount of responsibility given to sixth-formers, and the ways in which responsibility was accorded varied greatly. Systems of prefecture, where prefects were selected because of their personal qualities, were common. In these cases, the particular position of sixth-form pupils not selected for office was a matter of concern for some teachers in charge of sixth-formers. Those not selected were felt by some responders to be in an invidious position, and one teacher said, 'they tended to be the nervous rather than the wicked'. Another said 'unless it is absolutely impossible, we try to make all sixth-formers prefects'. In several schools there were no prefects as such. One headmaster said 'Prefects have very many duties. In many ways they run the school.'

Like so many other of the features examined in this study, the extent to which sixth-formers were given privileges varied enormously; in many cases they were merely nominal: wearing a distinctive tie or entering the school by the front door. In other instances, privileges of a more obvious nature existed—access to coffee making facilities, playing table-tennis and playing records in their own common-room and wearing fashionable clothes instead of a school uniform. Some schools encouraged a 'sixth-form college' atmosphere, with pupils free to come and go for classes. In one school where the college atmosphere was fostered, the teacher in charge of the sixth form said:

> 'We have gone as far as we can, I would not like it to go further while an example has to be given to the rest of the school. If we had separate sixth-form buildings for social purposes, the problem of smoking in front of the rest of the school would, for example, be less acute.'

The headmaster of an urban boys' school in a poor neighbourhood gave 'qualified approval' to the principle of student freedom. He considered his sixth-formers 'rather immature and lazy' and divided them between 'those who could be in a large room with a master present but relaxed atmosphere and those who could not'.

The physical facilities for the sixth form were as varied as their responsibilities and privileges. In many schools, they were considered hopelessly inadequate by their teachers, there being no place where the sixth could meet together as a form or socially, and in some cases the sole base of a sixth-former was a locker in a corridor. On the other hand, in one school a two-storey sixth-form block had just been provided by the local authority; it was designed for 100 pupils, and comprised a social and dining-room, lounge area, kitchen and cloakrooms, two study rooms, three tutorial rooms and an office study for the sixth-form teacher.

### The deployment of staff in comprehensive schools

In the first report (Monks, 1968) a study was made of which different year-groups and ages each member of staff taught. It was found that there was a tendency for graduates, men and experienced teachers to teach the older and more able pupils; the younger and less able pupils were more often taught by non-graduates and less experienced teachers. In the present report, one aspect of this is looked at again, using evidence derived from the timetable.

Interviews with school staffs showed that, in all but the smallest schools, the heads of subject departments recommended, or determined, which teachers should teach which pupils. In this study, teachers were considered, not in terms of their experience and qualifications, but in terms of their appointments. Pupils were considered in two categories:

(a) the most able, in terms of their teaching groups (streams or sets);

(b) their seniority in the school.

Sixth-formers in 11-18 schools, and fourth-formers in 11-16 schools were classed as older pupils. It was found that senior members of staff tended to take more of the work with abler and older pupils, and junior members of staff tended to take more of the work with less able and younger pupils (see Table 3.13). In large schools, where heads of subject departments were responsible for allocating staff to classes, there was some variation between departments, but even for practical subjects the pattern was the same. Some heads of departments spent all of their time teaching sixth-formers and top streams.

About one-quarter of the work in the large urban comprehensive school analysed in Table 3.13 could be classified as 'with sixth-formers and abler pupils'. Senior staff and heads of departments spent 37 per cent of their time with these classes but assistants with no posts of responsibility spent only 13 per cent. In every school for which data were examined, the pattern was similar. In a 13-18 school, with strong academic traditions, 46 per cent of the teaching was with 'sixth-formers and abler pupils'; senior staff spent 74 per cent of their time with these pupils and other staff spent 27 per cent of their time. In a banded 11-13 school where 41 per cent of the teaching was 'with the top band', senior staff and heads of departments spent 65 per cent of their time with these pupils—assistants without responsibility only 28 per cent.

TABLE 3.13: *Time spent by teachers with sixth forms and more able pupils in school 136 (percentages)*

| Nature of Appointment | Periods With Sixth Forms and Abler Pupils | Periods With Other Pupils | Total No. of Periods |
|---|---|---|---|
| Senior Staff and Heads of Depts. (24 Teachers) | 37 | 63 | 590 |
| Assistants with Graded Posts (11 Teachers) | 27 | 73 | 285 |
| Other Assistants (48 Teachers) | 13 | 87 | 982 |
| *Total* | 23 | 77 | 1857 |

## Libraries in comprehensive schools

The school library is an important adjunct to the educational provisions of the school. For schools serving pupils of a narrow age or ability range, the purposes of the library are usually reasonably well-defined and uncomplicated. The comprehensive school library has, however, to fulfil a variety of functions which may conflict. At one extreme, it may have to provide an environment where the individual can study in silence, using specialized texts which he can find and consult without supervision and advice. At the other extreme, it may be of prime importance to draw into the world of books those pupils who have little desire or home encouragement to exercise their reading skills. When a school is truly comprehensive its library may have to reconcile, with limited space, finance and facilities, both these extreme and contrasting purposes as well as other intermediate functions.

The library policy of 20 schools in the survey tended to be biased towards one or other of the extremes mentioned. Most former grammar schools tended to retain an academic atmosphere and a reference stock with a strong sixth-form flavour, usually requested or ordered by the heads of subject departments. Concessions to junior pupils usually consisted of rather restricted loan facilities. Former secondary modern schools tended to have a policy of introducing their pupils to library books at an earlier age and of providing reference material for topic work done in their subject classes. The established comprehensive schools attempted to fulfil both these roles, varying the atmosphere according to the requirements at different times of the day. This was not always ideal, and sometimes led to a situation where the sixth-formers were trying to study, and simultaneously there was the bustle of a junior class of 30 pupils selecting materials for topic work. Schools which tried to segregate and provide two or more libraries were faced with the difficulty of staffing and supervising them. In one school this led to a situation where the junior library was locked most of the time and was opened only for short periods each week to permit loan exchange.

The nature of a school library is often reflected in the list of periodicals available. A former grammar school with an academic library listed: *The Times, Guardian, Daily Telegraph, Yorkshire Post, New Society, New Statesman, New Scientist, Spectator, Economist, Time, Life, Atom, Project, Modern Language Review, Art and Design, Scientific American, Bunde, Paris-Match, Punch.*

A school with few academic pupils beyond the age of 13 listed: *Bradford Pictorial, Dalesman, Geographical Magazine, Commonwealth Today, Design, Discovering Art, Readers Digest, Woodworker, The Mouthpiece* (brass band), *Model Engineer, Football Monthly, World Sport, Sport and Recreation, Honey, Elle, Wild Life Observer, The Use of English.*

To staff the library, most schools relied upon members of the teaching staff with pupil helpers, but the staff usually had other commitments. In the Inner London Education Area schools visited each had a teacher-librarian and a full-time qualified librarian, with pupil assistants.

The School Library Association (1961) drew attention to the fact that 'the books needed to make a good collection . . . . are as many for a school of 150 as for one of 500 of the same age-range' and recommended that no school should have less than £50 a year for children aged 11 to 15 (1938 prices). The Association of Education Committees (1965) recommended an annual grant of £1 per head per annum for pupils aged 11-16, and £1.10.0. per head for pupils of 16 and over, with a minimum of £200.

To discern the actual amount of money spent on books was difficult, for many libraries received non-recurring capital sums, were subsidized by subject departmental funds, or were heavily supported by loans from the county library service. However, the average values for 20 libraries are shown in Table 3.14.

TABLE 3.14: *Average expenditure on school libraries*

| GRANT PER ANNUM | GRANT PER PUPIL | NO. OF VOLS. | VOLS. PER PUPIL | FLOOR SPACE |
|---|---|---|---|---|
| £438 | £0·478 | 7,354 | 7·7 | 1,754 sq. ft. |

The smallest annual grant was £30 (for a school of 330 pupils) but here support by loans from the county library was generous. The largest annual grant was £975 (for a school of 1,140 pupils) but here, again, there was additional support by loans from the county library.

If generalizations can be made, they are as follows:

1. most schools do less than they would like because of shortage of staff, space and money; overflow classes often have to use the library and, where study rooms have been provided as part of a library suite, they have often to be used permanently for other purposes;

2. many schools have not recognized or dealt with the conflicting roles a library in a comprehensive school must fulfil;

3. the best libraries, where staffing and finance are generous, compare favourably with good public libraries in suitability of stock, organization, staff, efficiency and accommodation.

### Summary

This chapter has surveyed the curriculum and guidance in a variety of schools. Throughout, attention has been directed upon the often conflicting aims of a comprehensive school, and the ways in which different schools have compromised between what is desirable and what is practicable.

1. The first pair of contrasting needs was that of postponement of specialization, as opposed to the need to adapt courses to meet the

varying capabilities and interests of different pupils. Early specialization can close certain careers to some pupils, but deferment of specialization can force the less able into continuing with a too academic curriculum and can slow down the progress of the more able. In many schools streaming and banding, adopted at an early stage and with little opportunity for transfer, reproduced a bi-partite selection system within one school. In others, a conscious effort to prevent this was made, particularly where similar, but not identical, parallel courses in option blocks made it possible for a pupil to select some subjects to GCE level, others to CSE or non-examination level.

2. The various ways of grouping pupils in the first year and in the fourth year were examined. It was found that ability grouping (whether in streams, bands or subject-sets) was generally imprecise, with considerable overlap of ability and attainment, as measured by our tests. The expected association between social class and ability is recorded. Supporters of comprehensiveness might draw attention to the fact that members of all social classes were found in all streams or bands. On the other hand, opponents might stress that the upper streams or bands had more pupils with parents in non-manual occupations than would be expected from a random distribution. The present follow-up of the careers of pupils tested in 1967/68 should add further to our knowledge of specialization and pupil mobility between teaching groups.

3. Size also illustrates the confliction of needs. In a small school it is difficult to provide the wealth of courses, studied at different levels to suit the needs of all pupils, which can be organized in a larger school. On the other hand, in the large school special measures have to be taken to cater for the welfare of pupils who may be lost in the supposedly impersonal environment.

4. Pupil welfare, particularly at the 'settling-in' stage, at the onset of specialization and in careers guidance, was briefly studied. In careers guidance it seems that the former grammar schools can learn from the experiences of staffs in former secondary modern schools and that if a gap exists, it is in the advice made available to the pupils who are neither in fourth-year leavers classes nor in the academic group staying on into the sixth form.

5. When the sixth form is reached, there is a further apparent conflict in some schools between the desire to retain an academic sixth of high standing and yet also provide for the needs of pupils of lesser ability who wish to stay on at school. Some schools uncompromisingly excluded non-academic pupils from the sixth form; others

imposed no restrictions. In some cases separate sixth-form courses were provided for non-academic sixth-formers; in others, option block systems, with major and minor subjects, enabled pupils to study a variety of subjects at different levels.

6. In some schools it was recognized that sixth-formers felt the need to be treated as young adults. Here, buildings, responsibilities and privileges were given to try to foster a 'sixth-form college' atmosphere. In other schools, less attention was paid to these social needs.

7. Conflicting needs are also illustrated by school library provision. A contrast was drawn between those schools where the library was seen as an academic reference library and those where it was viewed as a means of introducing all pupils to the world of books and their uses. In those schools where both these needs were recognized, the attempts to meet them were examined.

8. A study of the deployment of staff in comprehensive schools showed that in every school examined there was a strong tendency for senior staff and heads of departments to spend much of their time with older and more able pupils, while younger and less experienced teachers were frequently allocated to less able pupils and younger classes. This reached extremes in the subject departments of some schools, where some heads of departments taught only sixth-formers and top streams.

9. Schools which go comprehensive will have to arrive at their own solutions to the problems discussed in this chapter. These problems are provision for pupil mobility and of a wide range of optional subjects studied at various levels, concern for pupil welfare in settling down, choosing courses and careers, fostering a responsible adult atmosphere in the sixth, encouraging all pupils to use the library and other facilities and ensuring a balanced use of the most experienced staff. The compromises the schools will have to make may vary, and it is hoped that these descriptions of what some schools have done will help them.

# CHAPTER FOUR

# Attainment Survey

*by* P. EVISON

SO FAR this report has concentrated on the administration of the schools and their organization. We continue now by taking a closer look at the pupils. The heads and their staffs co-operated in this project not only by themselves completing questionnaires and being interviewed, but also by permitting, and often assisting or supervising, the administration of educational tests and questionnaires to their pupils.

This chapter describes the results of the attainment testing programme. The first, fourth and sixth years were selected for this—the first year to give a measure of the intakes to the schools, the fourth to assess the progress of all pupils, and the sixth to measure the composition and ability of those who had opted for a longer time at school.

## Tests used

While we were considering the tests for use with first- and fourth-year pupils, another of the Foundation's research teams, working on a follow-up of the Plowden Project, was also constructing a test battery for use with these same age groups in secondary schools of all types. The contents of this battery were substantially the same as we had planned and we adopted it for use with both year-groups. Two main advantages of this were that using the same tests for both the first- and fourth-year groups would facilitate comparisons in any longitudinal studies, and the Plowden Follow-up study would furnish up-to-date national norms for both year-groups.

The tests used at first- and fourth-year levels were therefore:

Test 1. *AH4 Group Test of Intelligence*[1] *Part II* (non-verbal section) (65 multiple-choice items requiring selection of correct shape or pattern in various situations, duration 10 minutes).

Test 2. *Watts-Vernon English Reading Test*[2] (extended by 10 extra

[1] Author A. W. Heim, MA, PhD   Published by NFER.
[2] Authors A. F. Watts, MA, DLit and P. E. Vernon, MA, PhD, DSc, and Department of Education and Science.

items) (45 multiple-choice sentence completion items, the correct word for completion of the sentence to be underlined, duration 15 minutes).

Test 3. *Vernon Graded Arithmetic/Mathematics Test*[1] (75 items, ranging from simple arithmetic to trigonometry and factorial number, duration 30 minutes).

This test battery, collectively known as test NF68, was suitable for pupils of a wide range of ability. The 10 extra more difficult items on the reading test were added to provide adequate coverage for the brighter fourth-year pupils and the appropriate adjustment was made to the time allowance.

An alternative version of the NF68 booklet was prepared for pupils whose first language was Welsh. In this version the AH4 (Part II) and the Graded Arithmetic/Mathematics tests were translated into Welsh, but the English Reading test was left unaltered, since it was felt that a translation of the latter test would have changed its nature and standard. Pupils in Welsh schools themselves selected the version of the booklet which they wished to attempt. These pupils were also asked to sit a separate Welsh reading test, the Welsh survey test NS71.[2]

For the first-year sixth-form pupils the CP66[3] (Schools Council Working Paper No. 21, 1969) test was used. This test provides a measure of general scholastic aptitude, using the principles of simple association, complex association, power of interpretation and thinking flexibility. Half of the 90 items in the test were designed to measure linguistic aptitude or verbal ability and the other half to assess quantitative thinking or mathematical ability. The time allowance was 50 minutes. Although national norms were not in existence for our precise age groups, the test had been used on GCE 'O' level and CSE candidates and data relating to these groups of pupils were available.

The tests were administered by the staff of the schools during the session 1967/68. The sixth-form testing was completed by December 1967 and, with the exception of a few schools, first- and fourth-year testing by March 1968. Completed test papers only were used in the analysis of the data, i.e. papers for which a mark for each individual test could be recorded.

[1] Author P. E. Vernon, MA, PhD, DSc Published by University of London Press Ltd.

[2] Prepared and standardized by HM Inspectorate for Wales, 1956/57.

[3] Authors L. S. Skurnik and I. M. Connaughton, NFER Examinations and Tests Research Unit.

**Test score results**

First-year pupils in 47 schools and fourth-year pupils in 48 schools attempted the NF68 test booklet. Included in the analysis are 8,074 first-year pupils in 45 schools and 7,606 fourth-year pupils in 46 schools. Of the two schools not included one had administered the arithmetic/mathematics test incorrectly and the other returned the completed booklets too late for inclusion in the analysis.

*First-year results*

Norms for the NF68 test booklet were obtained from the Plowden Follow-up study.[1] For this study a random sample of 836 first-year pupils, from all types of secondary school, completed the NF68 booklet in February—March 1968. Details of the mean scores and standard deviations for our own comprehensive sample and the 'Plowden' sample are given in Table 4.1 with the percentile distributions in Table 4.2.

The differences between the mean scores for the comprehensive and 'Plowden' samples for each of the sub-tests and the total are all very highly significant. Testing conditions for the 'Plowden' pupils may have been more favourable, since the number of pupils tested in any one school was small. However, the differences would seem to be too great to be accounted for by this factor alone, and since the 'Plowden' sample is nationally representative the comprehensive population seems to be lacking its full quota of higher ability

TABLE 4.1: *First-year NF68 mean and standard deviation scores*

|  | NON-VERBAL | | READING | | MATHE-MATICS | | TOTAL | | NUMBER OF PUPILS |
|---|---|---|---|---|---|---|---|---|---|
|  | *Mean* | *SD* | *Mean* | *SD* | *Mean* | *SD* | *Mean* | *SD* |  |
| 'Comprehensive' .. | 29·2 | 10·9 | 17·7 | 7·4 | 27·4 | 9·8 | 74·4 | 24·5 | 8,074 |
| 'Plowden' .. | 32·4 | 10·9 | 19·5 | 7·5 | 29·9 | 9·8 | 81·8 | 24·8 | 836 |
| *Max. Possible Score* | 65 | | 45 | | 75 | | 185 | | |
|  | t=7·93 | | t=6·59 | | t=6·89 | | t=8·19 | | |
|  | p<0·001 | | p<0·001 | | p<0·001 | | p<0·001 | | |

[1] Details of the original Plowden sample are given in Vol. 2 of the **Plowden Report**. In the follow-up study, the first- and fourth-year groups tested constitute approximately 85 per cent of the original year-group samples.

TABLE 4.2: *Percentile distributions for first-year NF68 scores*

| PERCENTAGE OF PUPILS | MARK SCORED LESS THAN: | |
| --- | --- | --- |
| | *'Comprehensive'* | *'Plowden'* |
| 10 | 40·9 | 47·3 |
| 20 | 53·0 | 60·3 |
| 30 | 61·8 | 68·4 |
| 40 | 69·0 | 76·3 |
| 50 | 75·2 | 83·4 |
| 60 | 81·2 | 90·1 |
| 70 | 87·2 | 96·0 |
| 80 | 93·9 | 103·6 |
| 90 | 102·7 | 113·8 |

pupils. These data are supported by the heads' estimates of the proportions of 'X' or higher ability[1] pupils in their 1965/66 intakes (Monks, 1968). This subject is discussed in more detail later.

The spread of school mean scores is very considerable, scores going from 55·4 to 89·8, a range of 34·4, which is more than one and a third of the standard deviation of all the first-year pupils tested. Only five schools had mean scores above the 'Plowden' mean score. The mean scores for schools grouped by various characteristics are discussed later.

The schools with the highest standard deviations were the junior high schools and the Welsh schools. A standard deviation gives an indication of the spread of ability, a relatively small standard deviation indicates a close clustering of the abilities of pupils, or a lack of pupils at the extreme ends of the ability scale. A good example of this is school 280, which has the smallest standard deviation and in which 75 per cent of the first-year pupils scored between 71 and 100.

*Fourth-Year Results*

The number of fourth-year pupils completing the NF68 test booklet was 7,606, distributed among 46 schools. The number of pupils in this age-group in the 'Plowden' sample was 849, and the mean scores and standard deviations together with the percentile distributions for these and the comprehensive pupils are given in Tables 4.3 and 4.4.

[1] 'X' pupils are defined as those pupils in the top 20 per cent of a national normal distribution of ability.

TABLE 4.3: *Fourth-year NF68 mean and standard deviation scores*

| | Non-Verbal | | Reading | | Mathe-matics | | Total | | Number of Pupils |
|---|---|---|---|---|---|---|---|---|---|
| | Mean | SD | Mean | SD | Mean | SD | Mean | SD | |
| 'Comprehensive' .. | 35·2 | 10·9 | 25·5 | 8·1 | 35·7 | 11·5 | 96·4 | 26·0 | 7,606 |
| 'Plowden' .. .. | 37·5 | 10·5 | 28·4 | 8·2 | 39·2 | 12·3 | 105·2 | 27·0 | 849 |
| *Max. Possible Score* | 65 | | 45 | | 75 | | 185 | | |
| | t=5·35 | | t=9·78 | | t=7·91 | | t=9·04 | | |
| | p<0·001 | | p<0·001 | | p<0·001 | | p<0·001 | | |

TABLE 4.4: *Percentile distributions for fourth-year NF68 scores.*

| Percentage of Pupils | Mark Scored Less Than: | |
|---|---|---|
| | *'Comprehensive'* | *'Plowden'* |
| 10 | 60·7 | 68·4 |
| 20 | 74·5 | 81·6 |
| 30 | 84·1 | 91·4 |
| 40 | 92·1 | 98·3 |
| 50 | 99·2 | 106·1 |
| 60 | 106·1 | 114·1 |
| 70 | 113·0 | 122·0 |
| 80 | 120·4 | 129·9 |
| 90 | 130·0 | 139·9 |

As with the first-years, the differences between the means for the two samples for the sub-tests and the total are each very highly significant. Again, for this age-group, there is a considerable spread of mean scores, ranging from 73·2 to 116·7; that is, a difference of 43·5 or more than one and a half pupil standard deviations. For this age group there are nine schools with mean scores above the 'Plowden' mean score.

*First-Year Sixth Results*

A total of 1,882 first-year sixth-form pupils in 43 schools sat the CP66 Aptitude Test. As the number of pupils in each school completing the test varied from nine to 124, it was not felt appropriate to compute a frequency distribution for each school separately.

As already mentioned, norms were not available for a first-year sixth-form age-group. The mean scores and standard deviations for 1,289 prospective GCE and CSE candidates, tested in 1966 (Schools Council Working Paper No. 21, 1969) are, however, given in Table 4.5, together with the results for our own comprehensive sample.

TABLE: 4.5: *Mean scores for CP66 aptitude test*

| POPULATION | MEAN | STANDARD DEVIATION | NUMBER OF PUPILS |
|---|---|---|---|
| Comprehensive .. .. .. | 51·8 | 15·8 | 1,882 |
| GCE .. .. .. .. | 56·2 | 13·3 | 584 |
| CSE .. .. .. .. | 39·3 | 13·2 | 705 |

The comprehensive sample sat the test in the Christmas term and therefore had an advantage of approximately six months over the GCE and CSE samples who sat the test in the summer term of their fifth year. The mean score of our sample lies between that of the GCE and CSE samples but is closer to the GCE score. The composition of sixth forms is discussed in more detail in Chapter 3.

TABLE 4.6: *CP66 population mean and standard deviation scores*

| | VERBAL | NON-VERBAL | TOTAL |
|---|---|---|---|
| Mean .. .. .. .. | 27·3 | 24·5 | 51·8 |
| Standard Deviation .. .. | 9·1 | 8·1 | 15·8 |

Again, there is a very considerable spread of mean scores between the schools. The scores range from 33·2 to 64·3, a range of approximately twice the overall standard deviation.

### 'X' and 'Z' pupils

The ability or quality of the intake of pupils into comprehensive schools is of some interest. In the earlier part of this study the heads were asked to estimate the percentage of very able or 'X' and less able or 'Z' pupils in their 1965/66 intakes, defined as those in the top or bottom 20 per cent of a normal national distribution. To enlarge upon this information the attainment survey results have been used to calculate the percentage of very able and less able pupils in the 1967/68 intakes to the sample schools. Pupils scoring more than the Plowden 80th percentile score are classified as 'X' pupils and those scoring less than the Plowden 20th percentile score as 'Z' pupils. The percentages of such pupils in each school are tabulated in Appendix A and compared with the heads' estimates of the corresponding percentages in the 1965/66 intake.

Heads' estimates and attainment survey results are available for 43 schools. For these schools, the two estimates for 'X' ability pupils agree to within five per cent for 29 schools, differ by between five and 10 per cent for nine schools and differ by more than 10 per cent for only five schools. In all but two of the cases where the difference between the estimates is more than five per cent it is the heads' estimates that are the greater. Thus it seems that there is a tendency for heads to over-estimate the number of able pupils in their schools. In the two schools where an underestimate was given, one head said that his intake was likely to improve due to secondary re-organization in his district.

The attainment survey shows that only 15 of the 45 schools completing the first-year testing had 15 or more per cent 'X' ability pupils in their intakes, and of these three had unexpectedly high proportions of more than 25 per cent.

Three types of school are, relative to the proportions in this sub-sample, over-represented in these 15 schools; they are junior high schools, schools with grammar schools in their origins and rural schools. On the other hand, the group includes none of the eight ILEA schools, nor any of the 14 schools in competition with grammar schools for the pupils in their intakes.

At the other end of the ability scale there are more discrepancies between the two estimates of 'Z' pupils. In only 19 schools do the estimates agree to within five per cent, eight differ by between five and 10 per cent and 17 differ by more than 10 per cent. In five of the eight instances where the estimates differ by between five and 10 per cent the heads' estimates of the percentages of 'Z' pupils are the greater, and it is interesting to note that four of these schools had grammar schools in their origins. In all other instances, however, where the two estimates differed by more than five per cent the heads had underestimated the proportion of 'Z' pupils in their schools.

One explanation for the apparently less accurate heads' estimates of

'Z' pupils is that although 'Z' was defined as the bottom 20 per cent of a national normal distribution of ability, there may have been an unconscious tendency to equate the term 'Z' with 'remedial'. This theory is supported by the fact that if, for the 20 schools where the heads' estimates seem low, the percentages of pupils scoring less than the Plowden 10th percentile score are taken, the agreement between the estimates is greatly improved. The position in these 20 schools then becomes: 11 pairs of estimates differ by less than five per cent, seven by between five and 10 per cent and only two by more than 10 per cent.

Using the proportions of 'Z' pupils from the attainment survey, 26 of the 45 schools had more than 25 per cent of 'Z' pupils in their 1967/68 intakes, and of these 17 had more than 30 per cent. Types of school over-represented at this end of the ability scale are schools of secondary modern origin only, ILEA schools, and those competing with grammar schools.

Looking at both ends of the ability-range simultaneously, nine schools had between 15 and 25 per cent of both 'X' and 'Z' ability pupils in their 1967 intakes, that is, only nine of the 45 schools could be said to have a more or less normal distribution of ability.

Summarizing these findings the following points emerge:

1. 'X' pupils are under-represented (only one-third of the schools completing the testing had more than 15 per cent of 'X' ability pupils in their 1967 intakes);

2. 'Z' pupils are over-represented (almost three-fifths of the 45 schools had more than 25 per cent of these pupils in their 1967 intakes);

3. only nine schools had what might be regarded as fully 'comprehensive' or balanced ability intakes in 1967/68. Of these, only seven schools can be considered fully comprehensive, since two are junior high schools of the type from which not *all* pupils transfer to senior high schools. (This type was stated in the Department of Education and Science Circular 10/65 to be acceptable only as an interim stage of development towards a fully comprehensive system);

4. none of the eight ILEA schools included in this sub-sample had more than 15 per cent of 'X' ability pupils, or less than 25 per cent of 'Z' ability pupils.

## Test score results for schools of various types

One of the aims of the attainment survey was to compare the attainment of pupils in schools of various types. The schools were grouped by age-range, competition with grammar schools, urban/ rural location, geographical region, origin and size. The significance tests used were either 't' tests (when only two groupings were involved, e.g. competition, or no competition, with grammar school) or, secondly, an analysis of variance. The test results of the groupings were obtained by using the mean scores of the schools; hence the mean for a particular group of schools is the unweighted mean of the means of the schools within that group.

No comparisons have been made between different years because of possible differences in the nature and quality of the intakes in successive school years, and possible policy changes. Such comparisons will be made when follow-up testing is carried out and results are available for the same pupils at different ages. Only in this way can valid conclusions be drawn about the relative progress of pupils in schools of various types.

The main problems in the interpretation of the results lie in the inter-relationships of the variables themselves; this makes it difficult to decide the extent to which any single school factor is responsible for the significant differences which are found. Some attempt is made below to outline these relationships.

*Age Range of Schools*

TABLE 4.7: *Total test scores and age range of pupils*

|  | FIRST YEAR (NF68) | | FOURTH YEAR (NF68) | | SIXTH YEAR (CP66) | |
|---|---|---|---|---|---|---|
|  | *Mean* | *No. of Schools* | *Mean* | *No. of Schools* | *Mean* | *No. of Schools* |
| JHS .. .. | 74·0 | 7 | 85·3 | 6 | — | — |
| SHS .. .. | — | — | 101·6 | 3 | 52·7 | 3 |
| 11–18 .. .. | 73·8 | 38 | 98·0 | 37 | 51·8 | 40 |
| *All Schools* .. | 73·9 | 45 | 96·6 | 46 | 51·9 | 43 |
|  | t<1 NS | | F=5·00 p<0·05 | | | |

The junior high school (JHS) group of seven comprises three schools where pupils may transfer to a senior high school at 14+, three where the age of optional transfer is 13+ and one where all pupils transfer to senior high schools at 13+. Of the three senior high schools (SHS) one receives pupils who opt to transfer at 14+ but in the other two all pupils transfer from junior high schools at 13+.

The table shows that the first-year means for the junior high and the 11-18 all-through schools do not differ. At the fourth-year stage, however, there is, as expected, a significant difference between the test scores for schools of various types, since the junior high schools contain only the residue of pupils not opting to transfer to senior high schools at 13 or 14+. The differences between the senior high schools and 11-18 schools are small for the sixth year and, since the number of senior high schools is so few, a significance test was not calculated.

## Competing with Grammar Schools

Since junior high schools do not have a full ability range of pupils in the fourth year and have no sixth-form pupils, they have been excluded from further analysis on these two age-groups.

TABLE 4.8: *Total test scores and competition with grammar schools*

|  | First Year (NF68) | | Fourth Year (NF68) | | Sixth Year (CP66) | |
|---|---|---|---|---|---|---|
|  | Mean | No. of Schools | Mean | No. of Schools | Mean | No. of Schools |
| Competing      .. | 69·1 | 14 | 91·8 | 12 | 43·9 | 11 |
| Not Competing.. | 76·0 | 31 | 101·1 | 28 | 54·6 | 32 |
| *All Schools*      .. | 73·9 | 45 | 98·1 | 40 | 51·9 | 43 |
|  | t=3·01 p<0·01 | | t=3·18 p<0·01 | | t=4·53 p<0·001 | |

The differences in mean scores are highly significant when the schools are divided according to whether they were competing with grammar schools, and this was so for test results in all three year-groups, the 'not competing' group of schools having the greater mean scores. None of the rural schools are in the competing group, but all ILEA schools included in this sample (eight in the first and fourth year and seven in the sixth year) fall into this competing category.

### Urban/Rural Location

When taking account of whether the schools were urban or rurally situated, it was decided to draw a distinction between the ILEA and other urban schools. Table 4.9 shows the schools grouped in this way

TABLE 4.9: *Total test scores and urban/rural location*

|  | First Year (NF68) | | Fourth Year (NF68) | | Sixth Year (CP66) | |
|---|---|---|---|---|---|---|
|  | *Mean* | *No. of Schools* | *Mean* | *No. of Schools* | *Mean* | *No. of Schools* |
| ILEA | 66·5 | 8 | 90·0 | 8 | 40·3 | 7 |
| Urban | 74·7 | 21 | 99·3 | 17 | 51·7 | 18 |
| Rural | 76·5 | 16 | 101·7 | 15 | 56·7 | 18 |
| *All Schools* | 73·9 | 45 | 98·1 | 40 | 51·9 | 43 |
|  | $F=5·75$ $p<0·01$ | | $F=4·65$ $p<0·05$ | | $F=19·15$ $p<0·001$ | |

There are significant differences between these groups of schools in all years, the first- and sixth-year differences being highly significant. The ILEA group means were the lowest in each of the three years. This was no doubt due, at least in part, to the fact that all the ILEA schools were in competition with grammar schools, but this was not so for any of the rural schools.

### Geographical Region

There were no significant differences between the means of the schools when grouped by region. The South group had the lowest mean scores in each year but it should be remembered that this group included all the ILEA schools.

TABLE 4.10: *Total test scores and geographical region*

|  | | FIRST YEAR (NF68) | | FOURTH YEAR (NF68) | | SIXTH YEAR (CP66) | |
|---|---|---|---|---|---|---|---|
|  | | *Mean* | *No. of Schools* | *Mean* | *No. of Schools* | *Mean* | *No. of Schools* |
| North .. | .. | 77·5 | 11 | 99·8 | 12 | 54·6 | 12 |
| Midlands | .. | 73·5 | 12 | 99·8 | 6 | 53·4 | 7 |
| Wales .. | .. | 72·6 | 7 | 101·1 | 7 | 53·4 | 10 |
| South .. | .. | 72·1 | 15 | 95·1 | 15 | 47·8 | 14 |
| *All Schools* | .. | 73·9 | 45 | 98·1 | 40 | 51·9 | 43 |
|  | | F=2·15 NS | | F=1·31 NS | | F=2·02 NS | |

## Origin

The classification here is by the origin or formation of the school: whether the school was newly founded when opened, formed from grammar schools (GS) only, from secondary modern schools (SM) only, or, lastly, formed by an amalgamation of grammar and secondary modern schools.

TABLE 4.11: *Total test scores and school origin*

|  | | FIRST YEAR (NF68) | | FOURTH YEAR (NF68) | | SIXTH YEAR (CP66) | |
|---|---|---|---|---|---|---|---|
|  | | *Mean* | *No. of Schools* | *Mean* | *No. of Schools* | *Mean* | *No. of Schools* |
| New .. | .. | 72·7 | 7 | 95·5 | 7 | 50·5 | 7 |
| GS .. | .. | 76·0 | 8 | 102·7 | 8 | 52·5 | 10 |
| SM .. | .. | 70·5 | 16 | 91·0 | 11 | 46·5 | 10 |
| GS+SM | .. | 77·1 | 14 | 102·9 | 14 | 55·6 | 16 |
| *All Schools* | .. | 73·9 | 45 | 98·1 | 40 | 51·9 | 43 |
|  | | F=2·25 NS | | F=5·04 $p<0·01$ | | F=3·07 $p<0·05$ | |

111

The slight differences between the means in the first year for these groups of schools were not significant, but at the older ages they were. It is tempting to make 'between-year' comparisons but, as already explained, such contrasts are not valid for a number of reasons.

*Size of School*

TABLE 4.12: *Total test scores and size of school*

|  | First Year (NF68) | | Fourth Year (NF68) | | Sixth Year (CP66) | |
|---|---|---|---|---|---|---|
|  | Mean | No. of Schools | Mean | No. of Schools | Mean | No. of Schools |
| 600 and under .. | 75·5 | 13 | 103·4 | 10 | 55·7 | 13 |
| 601–1200 .. | 73·4 | 22 | 96·3 | 20 | 50·8 | 20 |
| 1201 and over .. | 72·7 | 10 | 97·2 | 10 | 49·3 | 10 |
| *All Schools* .. | 73·9 | 45 | 58·1 | 40 | 51·9 | 43 |
|  | $F<1$ NS | | $F=2·71$ NS | | $F=2·26$ NS | |

Table 4.12 shows that although the pupils in small schools scored higher on average, size was not significantly associated with test score results for any of the year-groups. When the schools are divided into those with 600 or less pupils and the rest, however, the results for the fourth and sixth years just reach significance ($t=2·03$ and $2·10$ respectively, $p<0·05$).

*Summary*

Where significant differences occur the majority of the ILEA schools are within the group which produces the lowest mean scores. This is probably explained in some large measure by the fact that they are all in competition with grammar schools. These two associated factors seem to be responsible for most, if not all, the significant differences found.

**Test score results in Welsh schools**

The special arrangements made for Welsh-speaking pupils (i.e. those pupils for whom Welsh was the 'first' language) were outlined earlier. A second version of the NF68 booklet was produced in which the non-verbal ability and the Vernon Graded Arithmetic/Mathematics test were translated into Welsh while, for various special reasons, the Watts-Vernon English Reading test remained unaltered. The pupils themselves were allowed to select the version of the test booklet they wished to be tested in; in addition it was requested that all pupils should attempt a Welsh Reading test, the NS71.

Ten schools in Wales completed the first-year sixth-form testing and of these eight also completed the first- and fourth-year testing (although the booklets for one of these were returned too late to be included in the analysis). The two remaining schools were unable to administer the first- and fourth-year tests because of delays due to arrangements concerning the Welsh tests. Of the seven schools included in the first- and fourth-year analyses, two did not feel that the Welsh Reading test was appropriate, as their percentages of Welsh speaking pupils were small. One further school administered the Welsh Reading test to the least able first-year form only, while the remaining four schools administered it to all first- and fourth-years.

TABLE 4.13: *First-year NF68 scores*

| | NON-VERBAL | | READING | | MATHE-MATICS | | TOTAL | | NUMBER OF PUPILS |
|---|---|---|---|---|---|---|---|---|---|
| | *Mean* | *SD* | *Mean* | *SD* | *Mean* | *SD* | *Mean* | *SD* | |
| Welsh Schools (7) .. | 28·0 | 11·6 | 16·8 | 7·2 | 29·0 | 9·5 | 73·8 | 25·0 | 835 |
| English Schools (38) | 29·4 | 10·8 | 17·8 | 7·4 | 27·2 | 9·8 | 74·4 | 24·4 | 7,239 |
| *All Schools* (45) .. | 29·2 | 10·9 | 17·7 | 7·4 | 27·4 | 9·8 | 74·4 | 24·5 | 8,074 |
| | t=3·32 | | t=3·79 | | t=5·17 | | t=0·65 | | |
| | p<0·001 | | p<0·001 | | p<0·001 | | NS | | |

For first-year pupils, the difference in the Welsh and English schools' mean total scores is not statistically significant, although differences for the individual tests were all very highly significant. For the non-verbal and reading tests the English schools' mean scores were the greater, while the reverse was true for the mathematics test.

113

TABLE 4.14: *Fourth-year NF68 scores*

| | NON-VERBAL | | READING | | MATHE-MATICS | | TOTAL | | NUMBER OF PUPILS |
|---|---|---|---|---|---|---|---|---|---|
| | *Mean* | *SD* | *Mean* | *SD* | *Mean* | *SD* | *Mean* | *SD* | |
| Welsh Schools (7) .. | 36·9 | 11·4 | 26·0 | 8·8 | 39·2 | 11·4 | 102·1 | 27·4 | 759 |
| English Schools (39) | 35·0 | 10·8 | 25·4 | 8·1 | 35·3 | 11·5 | 95·8 | 25·8 | 6,847 |
| *All Schools* (46) .. | 35·2 | 10·9 | 25·5 | 8·1 | 35·7 | 11·5 | 96·4 | 26·0 | 7,606 |
| | t=4·38 | | t=1·34 | | t=8·93 | | t=6·04 | | |
| | p<0·001 | | NS | | p<0·001 | | p<0·001 | | |

In the fourth year, significant differences between the Welsh and English schools' mean scores were found for the non-verbal and mathematics sections and the total, all differences being very highly significant. The Welsh mean scores were the greater in each case.

TABLE 4.15: *First-year sixth CP66 scores*

| | VERBAL | | NON-VERBAL | | TOTAL | | NUMBER OF PUPILS |
|---|---|---|---|---|---|---|---|
| | *Mean* | *SD* | *Mean* | *SD* | *Mean* | *SD* | |
| Welsh Schools (10) | 28·6 | 8·5 | 25·6 | 7·8 | 54·2 | 14·5 | 260 |
| English Schools (33) | 27·2 | 9·1 | 24·3 | 8·1 | 51·5 | 15·9 | 1,622 |
| *All Schools* (43) .. | 27·3 | 9·1 | 24·5 | 8·1 | 51·8 | 15·8 | 1,882 |
| | t=2·44 | | t=2·48 | | t=2·75 | | |
| | p<0·05 | | p<0·05 | | p<0·05 | | |

The mean total scores for Welsh and English schools were significantly different, as were the means of the verbal and non-verbal sections.

*Welsh and English Reading Test Results*

The results for both Welsh and English Reading tests are tabulated in Table 4.16. Percentage mean scores have been computed as a basis for comparison, since the numbers of items in the tests are 45 and 35 for English and Welsh respectively. It must, however, be remembered that although the tests are of the same multiple-choice type, they are not matched for difficulty.

TABLE 4.16: *Welsh and English reading test scores*

**First year**

| School Code | % of Welsh† Speaking Pupils | Number of Pupils | English % Mean Score | Welsh % Mean Score |
|---|---|---|---|---|
| 349 | 100 | 92 | 39·8 | 65·1 |
| 338 | 80 | 77 | 25·3 | — |
| 270 | 50 | 154 | 35·8 | 37·7 |
| 371 | 30 | 40 | 34·4 | 29·1 |
| 375 | 10 | 188 | 37·6 | — |
| 374 | 5 | 141 | 39·6 | 14·6 |
| 356 | 5 | 132 | 43·3 | — |

**Fourth year**

| School Code | % of Welsh† Speaking Pupils | Number of Pupils | English % Mean Score | Welsh % Mean Score |
|---|---|---|---|---|
| 349 | 100 | 52 | 58·4 | 75·4 |
| 338 | 80 | 73 | 47·8 | — |
| 270 | 50 | 129 | 54·7 | 50·9 |
| 371 | 30 | 48 | 53·3 | 30·9 |
| 375 | 10 | 166 | 59·8 | — |
| 374 | 5 | 130 | 56·0 | 15·1 |
| 356 | 5 | 153 | 66·4 | — |

†Figures estimated by the DES, Cardiff.

The percentages of Welsh speaking pupils in each school are reflected in the Welsh Reading scores: as the proportion of Welsh speakers increases, so does the mean score of the school. An inspection of the Welsh Reading test papers for school 374 suggests that, for a large number of pupils, answers were arrived at by random selection of multiple-choice answers. In addition, some pupils did not attempt any questions—the school's mean score is, in fact, less than the mean expected score on a purely random selection of answers for the whole test.

Comparisons between first- and fourth-year groups are subject to the usual limitations, but it would appear that, in two schools, there is virtually no increase in attainment on the Welsh Reading test from first to fourth year while, in the remaining two schools the gain in scores between first and fourth years was considerable. School 338 administered the Welsh Reading test to the least able first-year form only and, for this form of 19 pupils, the mean percentage score was 45·1 as compared with an English Reading mean percentage score of 12·4.

The mean English Reading test scores for all schools, both English and Welsh, are 17·7 and 25·5 for first and fourth years respectively. Corresponding scores for Welsh schools only are 16·8 and 26·0. Three of the Welsh schools have means above the 'all school' average in both the first and fourth years.

TABLE 4.17: *Ranking of NF68 test scores for Welsh schools*

| | | RANK OF SCHOOL MEAN TEST SCORE† | | | | | | | |
|---|---|---|---|---|---|---|---|---|---|
| SCHOOL CODE | PERCENTAGE OF WELSH SPEAKING PUPILS | *First Year* | | | | *Fourth Year* | | | |
| | | Non-verbal | Reading | Mathematics | Total | Non-verbal | Reading | Mathematics | Total |
| 356 | 5 | 3 | 1 | 1 | 1 | 1 | 1 | 2 | 1 |
| 374 | 5 | 2 | 2 | 2 | 3 | 2 | 4 | 5 | 2 |
| 375 | 10 | 4 | 4 | 4 | 4 | 3 | 2 | 4 | 3 |
| 349 | 100 | 1 | 3 | 3 | 2 | 7 | 3 | 1 | 3 |
| 371 | 30 | 6 | 6 | 5 | 5 | 3 | 6 | 5 | 5 |
| 270 | 50 | 5 | 5 | 6 | 6 | 5 | 5 | 7 | 6 |
| 338 | 80 | 7 | 7 | 6 | 7 | 6 | 7 | 3 | 7 |

† Equal scores have been given the same rank.

From Table 4.17 it can be seen that high attainment in English Reading is, in general, coincident with high scores in other tests. It is also true that three of the four schools with the largest mean scores in each year-group are those with the smallest percentages of Welsh speaking pupils. However, the number of schools is too small to say whether or not this is anything more than chance.

The ranking for school 349 for the fourth-year non-verbal ability test appears to be out of keeping with the other rankings for this school. This is a small school and only 59 pupils in two forms completed the tests in the fourth year. An inspection of the mark lists for one of these forms suggests that there may have been a departure from normal test procedure in the timing, and this may account for the relatively low score. Alternatively, it is possible that this is a true score and that it is explained by the fact that this test is more a measure of ability as opposed to the others, which are more directly a result of classroom instruction.

## Summary

1. For each of the three year-groups, first, fourth and sixth, the range of mean test scores is very considerable.

2. The more able pupils are under-represented in the comprehensive schools in this sample; of the 8,074 first-year pupils tested only 12 per cent, compared with an expected 20 per cent, were found to be in the 'X', or able, category.

3. On the other hand, 28 per cent were found to be in the 'Z', or less able, category, whereas one would have expected only 20 per cent.

4. Competition from grammar schools was probably the cause of at least part of this imbalance in the intake of pupils, for it was more marked in urban schools, particularly in London, and less so in rural areas and Wales.

It is planned to add to this information after a further testing programme, part of which—the testing of fourth-year pupils who have stayed on into the sixth form—is already under way.

# CHAPTER FIVE

# Mixing and Friendship Choices

*by* T. KAWWA *and* T. S. ROBERTSON

THE AIM of this part of the study was to investigate how far pupils of different ability, social class, behaviour and race were mixing in the schools. It is relatively easy to make direct observations on small groups, but a study of the interactions of individuals in large groups requires other methods. Moreno (1960) and his early associates studied patterns of relationship among members of large groups by asking members to indicate the person, or persons, with whom they would like to associate. This sociometric technique has been widely applied in the United States, and Blyth (1960) has reviewed the use of the technique in this country. Kawwa (1963, 1965), Hargreaves (1967) and Ford (1969), among others, have used the technique in Britain. It was chosen for the present investigation as the most feasible way of studying the friendship patterns of large numbers of pupils in the limited time available.

In a sociometric test the subject is usually asked to write down in confidence the names of people he knows and with whom he would choose to do or plan a certain activity. In this investigation the criterion of choice was 'a very good friend'. This formed the principal part of the test and, together with other background data, was used for the analysis. The test also included a question intended to assess the pattern of rejections in the school: 'Which boy or girl in this school do you think it difficult to make friends with?' Throughout the questionnaire the boys were asked to name only boys and girls only girls.

The sociometric questionnaire[1] was developed and tried out before being produced in its finalized form. Where possible, administration of the test was done by the research worker himself to ensure uniformity, but in a few cases testing was undertaken by school staffs, in accordance with detailed written administrative instructions.

The analyses of these questionnaires proved difficult and time-consuming, for all the named pupils had to be identified in terms of

---

[1] This test and its instructions remain closed, and are not available for general use.

their attributes or characteristics and these matched against those of the responder. All choices were analysed in terms of in-group or out-group choices.[1] For example, if a pupil in Ability Group I chose as his best friend a pupil in Ability Group I, this was counted as an in-group choice, but if he chose a pupil in Ability Group II, this was counted as an out-group choice. When choices were classified in this way, chi-square tests of significance were calculated, to see whether the distribution of choices was likely to have occurred by chance or not.

In addition, an Index of Preference was computed to find out whether the in-group preferred itself to the out-group. If the IP is greater than one, then the members of the group prefer themselves to others; an index of less than one shows that the group prefers others to itself (Criswell, 1943).

In considering the results, the following criteria were studied:

1. the number of choices *received* by a group in relation to the number of pupils in the group; this measures the popularity of each group;

2. the number of choices *given* and whether there was a predominance of in-group or out-group choices.

### The popularity of different groups

As already mentioned, the number of choices received by pupils in a given group, divided by the number of pupils in that group, is a measure of the popularity of that group. (Since each pupil should record one choice, the average value should be 1. However, some pupils were absent and did not complete the questionnaire, while for others the data on certain pupil-qualities were not available or not classifiable, in this analysis the average value is therefore less than unity.)

Pooling the replies from eight schools, the number of choices received per pupil in each group is shown in Table 5.1.

It is clear that the more able pupils are on average more popular with fellow-pupils than the less able; the pupils in higher social classes more popular than those in lower; the better-behaved pupils more popular than the ill-behaved; and, lastly, in the unrepresentative sample of two schools where coloured pupils were in a small

---

[1] For a definition of the groups used in the analysis, see Appendix C. Although in the sociological sense these should be 'aggregates', the term 'group' is here used for convenience.

minority, white pupils more popular than coloured. This is true even though in most sub-groups (as will be shown later) there is a strong tendency for pupils to choose their good friends from the same sub-group. It means that when a pupil makes an out-group choice it is more likely to be 'upwardly' than 'downwardly' directed along each of the scales of ability, social class and behaviour. Moreover,

TABLE 5.1: *Relative popularity of different groups (eight schools)*

| | | | ABILITY GROUP | | | | |
|---|---|---|---|---|---|---|---|
| | | *I* | *II* | *III* | *IV* | *V* | *Total* |
| Classified Pupils | .. | 1095 | 1455 | 1438 | 1131 | 859 | 5978 |
| Choices Received | .. | 1044 | 1351 | 1257* | 900 | 644 | 5196 |
| Choices per Pupil | .. | 0·953 | 0·928 | 0·874 | 0·796 | 0·749 | 0·869 |

| | | | SOCIAL GROUP | | | | |
|---|---|---|---|---|---|---|---|
| | | *I* | *II* | *III* | *IV* | *V* | *Total* |
| Classified Pupils | .. | 145 | 1200 | 2441 | 1024 | 384 | 5194 |
| Choices Received | .. | 130 | 1005 | 1855* | 764 | 245 | 3999 |
| Choices per Pupil | .. | 0·896 | 0·837 | 0·760 | 0·746 | 0·638 | 0·770 |

| | | | BEHAVIOURAL GROUP | | | |
|---|---|---|---|---|---|---|
| | | *I* | *II* | *III* | *IV* | *Total* |
| Classified Pupils | .. | 4675 | 1001 | 107 | 48 | 5831 |
| Choices Received | .. | 4148 | 810 | 62 | 29 | 5049 |
| Choices per Pupil | .. | 0·887 | 0·809 | 0·579 | 0·604 | 0·866 |

| | | ETHNIC ORIGIN (TWO SCHOOLS) | | | | |
|---|---|---|---|---|---|---|
| | | *British White* | *European* | *Coloured* | *Other* | *Total* |
| Classified Pupils | .. | 2071 | 46 | 157 | 9 | 2283 |
| Choices Received | .. | 1844 | 45* | 120 | 5* | 2014 |
| Choices per Pupil | .. | 0·890 | 0·978 | 0·764 | 0·555 | 0·882 |

*Note*: All numbers of choices received, except those marked * differ significantly from the expected numbers.

the degree of popularity seems to be unrelated to the actual numbers in the group, at least insofar as the total population of these eight schools is concerned. Minority groups can be either popular, e.g. the 145 pupils in social class I, or less popular, e.g. the 92 ill-behaved pupils in groups III and IV.

What can be said with confidence about the findings for the total population can be said also about the pupils in each separate school, although there are certain reservations when the schools are considered individually, for the distributions did not differ from chance in a few cases.

### In- and out-group preferences

In Table 5.2, the distribution of friendship choices in one school made by pupils in different ability groups (the 'choosers'), is tabulated against the ability groups of the pupils whom they named as their very good friends (the 'chosen').

TABLE 5.2: *Distribution of choices among ability groups* (*School 314*)

|  | ABILITY GROUPS CHOSEN | | | | | | TOTAL CHOOSERS |
|---|---|---|---|---|---|---|---|
|  | *I* | *II* | *III* | *IV* | *V* | *Total Out-Group* |  |
| I | **268** | 73 | 16 | 4 | 1 | **94** | 362 |
| II | 74 | **193** | 48 | 21 | 3 | **146** | 339 |
| III | 23 | 58 | **156** | 51 | 15 | **147** | 303 |
| IV | 11 | 25 | 61 | **154** | 42 | **139** | 293 |
| V | 2 | 6 | 20 | 44 | **200** | **72** | 272 |
| *Total Chosen* | 378 | 355 | 301 | 274 | 261 | 598 | 1569 |

*Ability Groups Choosers*

$\chi^2_{16} = 1958 \cdot 0$, $p < 0 \cdot 001$

The 362 pupils in Ability Group I gave 268 choices to members of their own group and only 94 choices to members of all other groups. Thus, statistically speaking, there is a very highly significant chance of pupils choosing others from their own group. Each ability group in this school shows the same kind of in-group preference.

If the same pupils are classified by behaviour the same kind of pattern of choice emerges. This is shown in Table 5.3.

TABLE 5.3: *Distribution of choices among behaviour groups (school 314)*

|  |  | BEHAVIOUR GROUPS CHOSEN | | | | |
|---|---|---|---|---|---|---|
|  |  | *I* | *II* | *III and IV* | *Total Out-Group* | TOTAL CHOOSERS |
|  | I | **965** | 153 | 27 | **180** | 1145 |
| *Behaviour Groups Choosers* | II | 167 | **147** | 25 | **192** | 339 |
|  | III and IV | 35 | 34 | **12** | **69** | 81 |
|  | *Total Chosen* | 1167 | 334 | 64 | 441 | 1565 |

$$\chi^2_4 = 222 \cdot 77, \ p < 0 \cdot 001$$

Again, it is clear that the great majority of choices by pupils in Behavioural Group I were given to pupils in the same behavioural group, and that there was a highly significant in-group choice. However, the 339 pupils in Behavioural Group II gave *fewer* choices (147) to members of their own than to members of other groups (192 choices). Nevertheless, this still represents an in-group preference. for pupils in *other* behavioural groups are more numerous. If, in this case, the number of choices received is divided by the number of pupils in the groups the ratios of choices received/pupils in the group are $\frac{147}{339} = 0 \cdot 43$ for in-group choices and $\frac{192}{1226} = 0 \cdot 16$ for out-group choices. It is the number of choices given to members of a group, *in relation to the numbers of pupils in that group* which is important and if the friendship choices were being offered in a random fashion to pupils of all abilities we would expect these ratios to be the same.

Knowing that nearly all schools employ grouping systems based on ability (streaming, banding or setting), one would hardly expect choices to be offered in a random fashion, for pupils have more opportunities to mix with others nearer their own ability level. However, random choices for social class, behaviour and ethnic group are perhaps more likely, for the schools concerned do not deliberately segregate these pupils.

The preferences shown by members of different groups in each of the eight schools were calculated and are summarized in Tables 5.4, 5.5 and 5.6.

TABLE 5.4: '*In-group*' *preference and ability*

| SCHOOL | ABILITY GROUP | | | | |
|---|---|---|---|---|---|
| | *I* | *II* | *III* | *IV* | *V* |
| 072 | ( — in — ) | | in | in | in |
| 093 | in | in | NS | NS | in |
| 209 | in | in | in | in | in |
| 270 | ( — in — ) | | in | ( — in — ) | |
| 314 | in | in | in | in | in |
| 349 | ( — in — ) | | in | ( — in — ) | |
| 371 | in | in | in | in | in |
| 374 | in | in | in | in | in |

NS=no significant group preference

TABLE 5.5: '*In-group*' *preference and social class*

| SCHOOL | SOCIAL GROUP | | |
|---|---|---|---|
| | *I and II* | *III* | *IV and V* |
| 072 | in | NS | in |
| 093 | in | NS | NS |
| 209 | in | in | NS |
| 270 | in | NS | in |
| 314 | in | NS | NS |
| 349 | in | in | NS |
| 371 | in | † | † |
| 374 | in | NS | in |

NS=no significant group preference
†=numbers too small for analysis

123

TABLE 5.6: *'In-group' preference and behaviour*

| SCHOOL‡ | BEHAVIOURAL GROUP | | |
| --- | --- | --- | --- |
| | *I* | *II* | *III and IV* |
| 072 | in | in | † |
| 093 | in | in | † |
| 209 | in | in | † |
| 314 | in | in | in |
| 349 | in | in | † |

†=numbers too small for analysis
‡=numbers too small for analysis in 3 schools

In every *ability group* in all schools except one there proved to be an in-group preference. With the great predominance of streaming and setting this is not unexpected, but even in schools with a considerable amount of non-streaming, the preference pattern was still strongly for pupils to choose their best friends among those of similar ability. In every *behavioural group* where there were sufficient numbers of pupils to permit calculations to be made, the same picture was found; pupils for the most part chose their friends from those in the same behavioural group. In-group preference in *social classes* was less marked, but this may merely reflect the inadequacy of a classification by parental occupation to show accurately the differences in educational standards and attitudes which are important features of social class. The pupils in social classes I and II showed in-group preference in all schools, but in social classes III, IV and V this was not always the case. Fewer significant in-group preferences were noted in the manual than in the non-manual occupational classes.

In only one school were there sufficient non-British pupils to permit a study of ethnic preferences, and in this school British white pupils and coloured pupils both showed very highly significant in-group preferences.

Although nearly all groups showed in-group preference, there were differences in degree of inwardly-directed preference. The Index of Preference goes some way towards measuring this, but in the present study it was not possible to devise a satisfactory method of evaluating its precision. The Indices of Preference were calculated for each ability, social and behavioural group within each school and have been placed in rank order within each category in each school.

TABLE 5.7: *Rank order of index of preference*

| SCHOOL | ABILITY | | | | | SOCIAL CLASS | | | | | BEHAVIOUR | | |
|---|---|---|---|---|---|---|---|---|---|---|---|---|---|
| | *I* | *II* | *III* | *IV* | *V* | *I* | *II* | *III* | *IV* | *V* | *I* | *II* | *III* |
| 072 .. .. | 1 | 3 | 4 | 5 | 2 | – | 3 | 2 | 1 | – | 2 | 1 | – |
| 093 .. .. | 2 | 3 | 4 | 5 | 1 | 1 | 2 | 4 | 5 | 3 | 2 | 1 | – |
| 209 .. .. | 2 | 5 | 3 | 4 | 1 | – | 2 | 1 | 3 | – | 2 | 1 | – |
| 270 .. .. | 2 | 4 | 5 | 3 | 1 | 1 | 4 | 5 | 2 | 3 | 2 | 1 | – |
| 314 .. .. | 2 | 4 | 5 | 3 | 1 | 5 | 2 | 3 | 1 | 4 | 3 | 2 | 1 |
| 349 .. .. | 2 | 4 | 5 | 3 | 1 | 1 | 2 | 3 | 4 | – | 2 | 1 | – |
| 371 .. .. | 1 | 5 | 4 | 3 | 2 | – | 1 | 3 | 2 | – | 2 | 1 | – |
| 374 .. .. | 2 | 4 | 3 | 5 | 1 | 3 | 1 | 5 | 2 | 4 | 2 | 1 | – |

(Some groups omitted because of small numbers)

Despite the lack of a test of significance it is quite clear that ability groups I and V (that is, the most able and least able) are consistently more inward-looking than the middle ability-ranges, and the less well-behaved more inward-looking than the well-behaved.

There is a tendency for social class I and II to be more inward-looking than the other social classes.

## Between-school difference of inward-directed choices

Individual differences in the ways in which responding schools interpreted the instructions on providing pupil data, differences in response rates, and systematic difference in local employment patterns, all combine to make between-school comparisons difficult. For example, although schools were asked to divide the pupils by ability into five groups with approximately equal numbers in each, few schools actually did this. Also, using the Registrar-General's classification of social class, the figures for social class II in rural schools are misleadingly high, for farmers of small and large holdings can hardly be compared with the urban class II parents, who are for the most part clerical workers.

An overall Index of Preference for each school on each pupil dimension has been calculated. These indices are shown in Table 5.8.

Taking into account the difficulties of making comparisons, all that can be said is that there are large between-school differences in the degree of inward-directedness on ability, but greater uniformity for social class and behaviour. In some schools where there is strong

TABLE 5.8: *Overall indices of preference in separate schools*

| SCHOOL | ABILITY | SOCIAL CLASS | BEHAVIOUR | ETHNIC ORIGIN |
|--------|---------|--------------|-----------|---------------|
| 072 | 2·40 | 1·21 | 1·69 | 1·07 |
| 093 | 1·58 | 1·03 | 2·59 | 3·25 |
| 209 | 2·08 | 1·29 | 1·52 | 0·75 |
| 270 | 2·04 | 1·28 | 1·73 | — |
| 314 | 6·38 | 0·99 | 1·20 | 1·06 |
| 349 | 2·28 | 1·25 | 1·34 | — |
| 371 | 3·16 | 1·14 | 0·98 | — |
| 374 | 5·12 | 1·29 | 1·65 | 0·98 |

in-group preference for ability there is little apparent in-group preference on social class (school 314); in other cases (school 093) comparatively low in-group preference on ability accompanies low in-group preference on social class.

Ford (1969) studied the social class in-group preferences of children in different types of school (grammar, comprehensive and secondary modern school). Using small numbers of pupils, she reached a tentative conclusion that in streamed schools children appeared to prefer to mix with those from similar social background. This conclusion is supported, but at the same time our results show that a considerable amount of social class mixing does, in fact, occur. A fuller analysis of the data, at present under way, should add to our knowledge of the relationship of social mixing to educational grouping in comprehensive schools.

**Summary**

Nearly every pupil in eight (largely dissimilar) comprehensive schools completed a questionnaire in which he was asked, among other things, to name a very good friend. All pupils were classified according to ability, social class, behaviour and ethnic origin. A study was made of the popularity of the various groups, and of the extent of in-group and out-group preference in the choice of the pupils' best friends.

It was found that:

1. The more able pupils were generally more popular with their colleagues (i.e. the total population of pupils in the school) than the less able.

2. Pupils with fathers in the higher social classes were generally more popular with their colleagues in school than those from lower.

3. The better-behaved pupils were generally more popular with their colleagues than the less well-behaved.

4. The degree of popularity seems not to depend on the size of the group; minority groups can be popular or unpopular.

5. Minor differences from these patterns found in a few individual schools may not be significant.

6. There is a strong tendency for pupils to choose their best friends from among pupils in the same ability, social, behavioural or ethnic groups.

7. This in-group preference appears more strongly in ability and behavioural groups than in social groups.

8. Although nearly all groups into which pupils were classified are found to be inward-looking, some groups are more inward-looking than others:

(a) the most and least able pupils seem to be more inward-looking than the pupils of the middle range of ability;

(b) the pupils whose parents are in non-manual occupations tend to be slightly more inward-looking than those whose parents are in manual occupations;

(c) the less well-behaved pupils are more inward-looking than the well-behaved.

9. Considerable differences in the degree of inward-direction of friendship choice occur in different schools, particularly so far as ability groups are concerned. These cannot be explained at present. They do not seem to be related, at least not closely, to the degree of streaming, but all schools studied had some streaming or setting of pupils.

It is hoped to extend this study of friendship patterns at the next stage of this project with greater reference to the internal organization of the schools.

# CHAPTER SIX

# Voluntary Extra-Curricular Activities

*by* M. I. REID

A STUDY of extra-curricular activities might seem to require some justification if such activities are viewed as peripheral rather than essential aspects of school life. Several considerations prompted their investigation in the second stage of this project.

First, such activities provide a context for the meeting of pupils of different ages, abilities, social groups and attitudes. In schools which are fairly rigorously streamed, the possibilities for an increased integration of the school community are clear, and in streamed and partially-streamed schools alike, social contact among pupils outside a formal classroom situation might be of considerable importance. Indeed, if we want to know the degree to which the comprehensive school achieves integration among its varied intake of pupils, a study of pupil participation in activities seems essential.

Secondly, the Central Advisory Council for Education, under the chairmanship of Sir John Newsom, reported findings which it was considered could be profitably followed up. Its report *Half our Future* (1963), drew attention to the fact that the majority of pupils at the ages of fourteen and fifteen spend no more time in school than they did at seven. Also, 'a disturbing number', the report states, 'seem to leave school under-equipped in skills, knowledge and in personal resources. A characteristic complaint of this group is that they are bored . . . .' Extra-curricular activities provide a means of meeting the special interests of pupils and of equipping them with additional skills and information. The boredom which the so-called Newsom pupils displayed may show itself in a lack of involvement in such activities, and their inadequacies may be underlined by their failure to take advantage of these opportunities. Because of this, it is valuable to assess the extent to which pupils take part in activities, and to study the relative participation of boys and girls of different ages, abilities and backgrounds.

Finally, in view of trends towards a shorter working week and the increasing use of mechanical equipment in the home, it seems probable that schools will want to educate their students in the use of

128

leisure time. A study of aspects of such education as it exists today might provide useful information for schools seeking to develop their extra-curricular programme.

## The scope of the study

The term 'voluntary extra-curricular activity' is not easily defined in all schools. The decision as to whether activities were run on a voluntary basis in a particular school or whether a particular pursuit was extra-curricular relied ultimately on the discretion of the researcher. In one school, for instance, activities occurred mainly in curricular time, so that the data could not be used to indicate the degree of pupil participation, although it provided material for an analysis of pupil preference in a forced-choice situation. In other schools activities such as social-service projects formed part of a curricular course, although they overflowed into extra-curricular time. These were not included when assessment was made of the number of activities pupils pursued. Generally, activities were considered to be 'voluntary' and 'extra-curricular' when they occurred wholly or mainly outside 'timetabled time' when they did not constitute part of any curricular course and when they were undertaken initially at the pupil's own choice. Our criterion of an 'activity' depended to a great extent upon what the pupils themselves considered as such, in terms of a club, society, group or team to which they could affix a label. The participation which we have studied and measured may therefore not take account of the sporadic and less formal types of extra-curricular activity found in some schools.

The first stage of the research into comprehensive education furnished information on the range of activities pursued in 331 schools, together with estimates by the heads of pupil participation with reference to ability and age. Information was also collected about the teachers who took part in such activities in terms of level of appointment, qualifications, sex and years of teaching experience (Monks, 1968). Of the data collected in the more detailed Stage II inquiry it has been possible at this stage to examine only part, under the following headings:

1. school policy towards extra-curricular activity: a description of the functions of such activity as perceived by heads, and of the methods used by schools to organize and publicize their extra-curricular programmes;

2. pupil participation in activities: a detailed look at the

E

characteristics of participant and non-participant pupils in terms of their year-group, sex, ability and social class;

3. environmental factors affecting participation: an examination of factors of possible relevance to participation, such as time spent on travelling, homework, parental attitudes and factors relating to the internal and external school environment.

Information was collected through a structured interview with the heads of 31 of the 59 schools, and in 17 of these an intensive study of pupil participation was made, with each pupil completing a questionnaire on his activities. The schools were selected on the basis of their providing sufficient activities for pupils to have a real opportunity to participate, of their furnishing the necessary data about year-groups, ability, and parental occupations, etc. and of their agreeing to administer questionnaires to their pupils. Within these limits we tried to ensure that schools of various sizes, origins, intakes, locations and site-structures were represented, as well as both mixed and single-sex schools.

All interviews and instruments were completed in the Spring term so that staff and students had had time to decide upon extra-curricular commitments at the beginning of a new school year. There were strong reasons for avoiding the Summer term, with the added duties placed on staff at this time by external and school examinations. and the disruption of pupils' usual patterns of extra-curricular activity, by social and sporting functions.

## School policy towards extra-curricular activity

### 1. *Function*

Heads were asked to give their views on the functions of extra-curricular activity and their replies have been classified into groups which are listed below.

| FUNCTIONS | No. of Heads Mentioning (Total=31) |
|---|---|
| 1. Promotion of social cohesiveness . . . . | 20 |
| 2. Fostering staff-student relationships . . | 13 |
| 3. Promotion of interests/hobbies and education for leisure . . . . . . . . . . | 11 |
| 4. Extension of curricular activities . . . . | 10 |
| 5. Broadening the basis of education (through the provision of studies *not* included in the curriculum) . . . . . . . . . . | 9 |

6. Helping towards social education and personal development  .. .. .. ..        7
7. Providing opportunities for pupils to exercise choice  .. .. .. ..        7
8. Promotion of public/community relations ..
9. Keeping pupils occupied  .. .. ..
10. Combating cultural deprivation in neighbourhood  .. .. .. .. ..
11. Providing opportunities for pupil leadership
12. Giving the pupil interests which he can continue after leaving school  .. .. ..
13. Providing opportunities for less able pupils
14. Enabling more extensive use of school facilities
15. Providing the occasion for an inter-disciplinary approach to school work  .. ..
16. Providing an example of 'staff-giving'  ..
17. Providing opportunities for special ventures and occasions ..  .. .. .. ..

given by
5 or
fewer heads

Replies classed under 'social cohesiveness' include those which referred to activities as 'building up the corporate life of the school' in general terms, as well as those which were more specific in stating that activities were a means of 'breaking down barriers created and reinforced by streaming and setting'.

The main point to emerge from comments allocated to the second, staff-student relationship category was that clubs and societies afforded the opportunity for a qualitatively different relationship between teaching staff and pupils than was possible in the classroom. An interesting remark here was made by the head of a large comprehensive school in a 'poor' area, stressing that 'where good adult/child relationships in a neighbourhood are lacking, out-of-classroom contact with the teaching staff provides pupils with valuable experience in forming relations with adults on a non-authoritarian basis'.

Over a third of the heads saw activities as a means of introducing students to new interests and to profitable ways of spending leisure time. 'Extra-curricular activities', in the words of one headmaster, 'are really instruction periods in the use of leisure'. Leisure education was advocated for a variety of reasons—because it provided the opportunity for the pupil to 'extend his potentiality', 'to express himself fully', and 'to experience the fullness of life'. One headmaster emphasized the need for schools to cater for the great variety of pupil interests and to avoid rigid concepts of what was 'worthwhile'—'it

131

doesn't matter what it is as long as it is something' were the words he used. Important points emerging from some interviews were that schools could give practical help by offering special facilities and experienced tuition to pupils, and could organize many interests and hobbies which could not adequately be followed by the pupil in isolation.

Ten heads saw the extension of curricular subjects as a function of activities; their comments were grouped together because they stressed the need for activities to be linked to classroom instruction: 'societies exist for educational purposes—they are an extension of the curriculum'; 'pupils need a follow-through after school on what they've heard in class—an extension of classroom specialization is required'. Those replies classified under the heading 'broadening the basis of education', on the other hand, stressed that extra-curricular activities provided the opportunity for pursuits which the normal school curriculum did *not* allow and enabled the school to impart a wider range of skills, and combat the 'narrowness' of the curriculum.

Providing the pupils with an opportunity to exercise choice was seen by some heads as an important aspect of activities: 'there is *educational* value in the element of free choice involved', and 'activities provide an experience of *real* permissiveness. A child may join and leave as he wishes—it's probably his first real choice situation in school'.

Activities were seen by five heads as increasing the school's prestige among parents and public. An interesting comment came from the head of a former secondary modern school in the process of adapting to a junior high school: 'Extra-curricular activities are a status symbol. They raise the status of a modern school'. Four other heads interviewed saw activities as a means of a school enriching its surrounding community. The head of a South London comprehensive school located in a neighbourhood of 'cultural deprivation' considered that in such an area, his school had vast resources and therefore a responsibility to provide as full a programme of activities as possible.

One further category—'keeping the child occupied' requires elaboration. The comments in this classification showed concern that many pupils had little or nothing to do after school and had no adult supervision between four o'clock and the time their parents returned from work.

The heads, then, attributed a wide variety of functions to voluntary extra-curricular activities; most commonly they saw them as a means of developing social cohesiveness, of fostering good staff-student relationships, of educating pupils for leisure and of supplementing curricular instruction or providing pursuits which the strictures of the curriculum did not allow. Although the number of schools studied was small, interesting trends were found. The heads of the larger comprehensive schools and of schools situated in urban areas mentioned functions concerned with *relationships*—both among the students themselves and between the staff and the students—more frequently than heads of the smaller and rural schools. In the former types of school, activities may be of particular value in bringing together pupils and teachers. A greater proportion of heads of new than adapted schools said that these activities were a useful means of integrating the school community and, in addition, heads of schools where the buildings were scattered on two or more sites spoke of the social cohesiveness function.

Several other points of interest emerged. The development of staff-student relationships was given as a function of activities more frequently by heads of schools with a low intake of the more able pupils (the 'X' pupils referred to earlier in this report) than by those of schools more generously endowed with such pupils. The promotion of interests and hobbies and the education of the student for leisure was considered a function of out-of-classroom activities more frequently by heads of rural than urban schools—probably because in the rural community the school is more likely to be the sole centre where instruction and facilities for leisure-time pursuits are available. Finally, the tendency to see activities as school-subject-based and supplementary to curricular instruction was more characteristic of heads of comprehensive schools derived from grammar schools than of heads of schools adapted from other forms of secondary provision or new schools.

Three of the heads doubted the value of extra-curricular activities, either for the individual pupil or for the school as a whole. The head of a junior comprehensive school said that in these first three years a firm foundation had to be laid for the upper school and was concerned lest too much time be given to activities. Similar concern was expressed by the head of a rural school in Wales: 'We must not forget the pressures of academic studies, and in the end a child is interested in a good "O" and "A" level'. Another head, although stressing the value of activities generally, queried their function in the specific case of remedial groups: 'Most activities', he pointed out, 'require skill. What is a suitable activity for a "remedial" child to stay behind for?'

Finally, a number of heads doubted whether a distinction between

133

curricular and extra-curricular activity was a real or desirable one in modern education. The whole concept of extra-curricular activity was labelled by one headmaster as a 'grammar school idea', and another head felt that a clear-cut distinction would only occur where the curriculum was not free and flexible, and where a break from 'rigid' lessons was necessary.

## 2. Organization

Three aspects of the organization of activities in schools were reviewed: methods of allocating time, units used as focal points, and procedures employed for their initiation and organization. Fairly general practices were found in each of the three areas; of particular interest, perhaps, are those schools not conforming to the common pattern, either through the need to meet a specific problem or through a desire to experiment.

(a) *Time allocation.* The 31 schools may be divided into three categories in their time allocation: those where no curricular time was made available for activities; those where some curricular time was allocated, and those where the programme of lunch-hour and after school clubs and societies was supplemented by evening activities.

Nineteen of the 31 schools are classed in the first category, with activities taking place at the traditional times, that is during a lunch-hour of normal duration (up to 70 minutes), and at the close of afternoon school. One-third of the rural schools and almost three-quarters of the urban schools allocated activities to these times.

Seven schools made curricular time available for activities, and where this was done one of two methods was employed. The first, found in four schools, was to extend the lunch break to a period of one and a half hours. The second, occurring in three schools, was to allow normal timetabled periods for activities, either for the whole school population or for selected year-groups. In one such school in a rural area, the major part of all extra-curricular activity occurred during one 45-minute period in a six-day timetable. The second school, again rurally situated, devoted a double period on one afternoon each week to activities for its fourth-, fifth- and sixth-form pupils. The third school, a large urban comprehensive, allocated one period per week to activities organized throughout the school on a year basis; this was supplementary to lunch hour and after school meetings. (Two further schools planned to introduce activities in curricular time in the following session—for pupils in the lower ability forms in the one instance and for first- and second-year pupils in the other.)

Four of the 31 schools supplemented daytime activities with evening youth clubs, admitting school members only in three cases, and being organized in all four schools by members of the school staff. Three of these four schools, as might be expected, had urban catchment areas, while the one rural school was able to meet transport problems with the help of a local education authority vehicle. Five other heads expressed a wish to see the introduction of evening activities in some form in their schools. Altogether, nine of the 31 heads interviewed had either already introduced, or wished to introduce activities in the evening. This is of interest in view of the Newsom proposals for an extended school day.

One school was exceptional in that it followed none of the procedures outlined above. In the 1967/68 session it introduced a 'reorganized' school day, with no lunch break, and ending at 2.50, so making the major part of each afternoon available for clubs and societies.

The time allocation for activities in schools may be summarized as follows:

(i) the 'traditional' situation—activities in the lunchhour and after school (19 schools);

(ii) as above, with the addition of an evening youth club (4 schools);

(iii) activities taking place mainly in an extended lunch hour (4 schools);

(iv) some or all activities taking place in curricular time for some or all sections of the school (3 schools);

(v) activities taking place after school only, with the school day ending at 2.50 p.m. (1 school).

Schools in rural areas showed a greater tendency to depart from the traditional system. Of the nine rurally located schools, two were operating an extended lunch hour and a third was about to introduce it. A further two made curricular time available and one more was planning this for the following school year. An evening youth club supplemented the usual extra-curricular programme in another. In fact, only two of the nine rural schools were not either operating or proposing to operate some system of time-allocation other than the traditional 'lunch hour and after school' system. This compares with the majority of the urban schools which neither operated nor proposed to operate anything other than the traditional system. Rurally located schools seem to find that the traditional procedure of allocating activities to a lunch break of up to 70 minutes and to time after school meets the needs of their pupils less adequately than is the case in urban schools.

(b) *The school units around which activities were centred.* Heads were asked to specify the administrative, social and tutorial units in their schools which served as centres for the organization of voluntary extra-curricular activities.

Twenty-three of the schools in this sub-sample operated house-systems but, perhaps surprisingly, these were used only occasionally as focal points for activities. In five instances no extra-curricular activities of any kind were attached to the house unit and in a further 12 schools it was used only for the organization of occasional competitive sport. In only six schools was the system employed in any regular way to provide organizational units for a variety of activities, of which competitive sport formed only one aspect. In one of these six schools, houses combined to hold informal house evenings twice a week, with a varied programme of activities. In another the houses concentrated on a particular kind of activity—fund-raising for charity and community projects, in connection with which a regular series of events took place. In three of the remaining schools, the house system was used to operate a programme of musical and dramatic activities and in the fourth it was the centre of activities ranging from indoor games to theatre visits and fell-walking.

House-centred activities were always complemented by those organized around horizontal school units and/or by activities which were school-based. The units and combinations of units used by the 30[1] schools are detailed below, together with the average size of the schools in each group:

| UNITS AROUND WHICH ACTIVITIES WERE ORGANIZED | NUMBER OF SCHOOLS | SIZE/ MEAN SIZE |
|---|---|---|
| Whole school only | 4 | 719 |
| Whole school + year-groups | 1 | 550 |
| Whole school + sections of school | 14 | 946 |
| Whole school + sections of school + year-groups | 7 | 1106 |
| Sections of school + year-groups | 2 ⎫ | |
| Year-groups and form-groups only | 1 ⎬ | 1668 |
| Sections of school only | 1 ⎭ | |

The four schools in which all activities were organized on a whole-school basis tended, predictably, to be the smaller ones, with three

[1] The one school in which nearly all activities were timetabled is not included.

having fewer than 700 pupils. The most frequent combination, found in 14 of the schools was that of the whole school and sections of it; this method of organizing activities appeared to be unrelated to school size, which varied from 390 pupils at one extreme to 1,618 at the other. Some schools, as well as having activities centred round the whole school and school-sections, also used year-groups, and these schools were on average larger than those using the whole school and school-sections only.

A few schools had no activities organized on a whole-school basis and used only school divisions—forms, year-groups or sections. The average size of these schools was 1,668 pupils.

The evidence from this small survey, then, is that the larger the school, the greater the use of school divisions as centres from which extra-curricular activity can be developed. In some of the smallest schools such divisions were not employed at all and all activities were whole-school based. At the other extreme, four of the largest schools found activities organized for the entire school population impracticable and made use not only of the school section as a unit for organizing activities, but also of the smaller year—and in one instance form—groups. The most common pattern was one between these two extremes, with some activities being whole-school activities and others being centred round sections of the school.

(c) *How activities were initiated and organized.* How frequently did activities arise from pupil initiative and how often did the impetus come largely from the teaching staff?

In almost two-thirds of the 30 schools, most or all activities were initiated by the staff; in a further five, the heads said that activities arose from a combination of staff and pupil initiative, with the interests of the one meeting the needs of the other. In four schools only were most activities pupil-initiated and, with one exception these were senior comprehensive schools. To provide more specific information, the heads were later asked about those activities which had originated within the last school year and how these had been initiated. Of a total of 67 new activities listed by the 28[1] heads who were able to reply to the question, 43 had arisen through the enthusiasms of members of the teaching staff, and the rest had started either from pupil initiative or from a combination of staff and pupil initiative.

A study was made of the organization of the principal activities in

[1] Two of the 30 heads who were asked how activities in their schools originated felt unable to answer the question with any degree of accuracy. The school where activities were timetabled is again not included in this section.

each of the 30 schools, using heads' assessments of which these were in terms of meeting frequency and size of membership. To ensure that the full range was represented, heads were asked to give the main activity in their schools in each of the following categories of activities: outdoor (other than school teams); neighbourhood and social work; debating and discussion; arts-subject based; science-subject based; arts and crafts; music; drama; other indoor activities (e.g. chess, badminton, etc.) and, finally, those activities connected with the Duke of Edinburgh Award Scheme. Schools were often deficient in some categories but had several thriving activities in others and, where this occurred, more than one activity per category was studied. The number of 'main activities' thus selected averaged 8·5 per school. In each case, the teachers organizing the activities were interviewed and asked about the use of pupils in activity-organization. Out of the total 256 activities surveyed in this way, in 150—some 60 per cent—the teaching staff assumed total responsibility for all aspects of organization. Only one instance in this whole study was found of an activity which was entirely pupil-organized to the extent that the pupils themselves had to be interviewed in place of the teaching staff.

A greater proportion of activities were partly pupil-run in those schools with a relatively high (20 per cent and over) intake of 'X' or able pupils and also in boys' as compared with girls' and mixed schools. Five of the 30 heads expressed the opinion that pupils should initiate and organize more of their schools' extra-curricular programme.

### 3. *How Schools Publicized Their Extra-Curricular Programme*

The last aspect of general school policy towards voluntary extra-curricular activities to be examined was the way schools publicized them and emphasized their importance to their students. The most common methods were through the school assembly and the general school noticeboard. One-third of the schools studied used a combination of these two methods, with no other forms of publicity. The remaining schools supplemented or replaced the two methods above by notices given in house or year assemblies or by those displayed on form, year, house or special society noticeboards, or by public address system announcements. Ways of making publicity more effective included the use of regular (weekly or fortnightly) circulars to pupils, and in one instance to parents, about forthcoming events. Generally, the larger schools and schools with peculiar communication problems, such as the separate-site schools, employed a greater variety of publicity methods than the smaller and single-site schools.

The ways in which schools brought the 'achievements' of any particular activity group to the notice of the school population as a whole were also looked at. The most common procedures were announcements in assembly (28 schools), at speech day (23 schools), in the school magazine (18 schools) and at the end of term assembly (14 schools), but it is the departures from these normal practices which are perhaps of greater interest. In five schools regular bulletins were produced with descriptions of recent activities, while in several others it was policy to seek press coverage for as many of the schools' activities as possible. This was seen not only as a means of making extra-curricular activities appear more prestigious to the student, but also as a way of integrating the school more closely with its surrounding community. Two more schools aided publicity by ensuring that their 'unattached' pupils were given opportunities to see school clubs and societies in action.

Two less direct ways of stressing the importance of activities to pupils were also studied: the degree and nature of the head's personal involvement in activities and the methods used to record pupil participation. Heads were involved personally in clubs or societies in only five schools and these tended to be the smaller ones (average size 653 pupils). Most heads, however, acted as general co-ordinators of extra-curricular pursuits in their schools and either constructed the extra-curricular programme personally (17 schools) or convened 'cabinets' of senior teaching and/or house staff at the beginning of the school year to deal with this (six schools). Commonly, heads visited activities, but few set aside time specifically for this, and nine out of 31 estimated that they made such visits rarely, if at all.

All except four schools recorded pupil participation in activities in some way, using the record card (26 schools), the school report to parents (24 schools) and the leaving testimonial (30 schools), with variation in the amount of detail included and in the procedures used to obtain the necessary information. Most schools detailed activities fully on record-cards, but in only a third did the design of reports to parents permit their full specification. In the remaining schools using reports to record activities, these were mentioned either in the general concluding comment or in the remarks of subject teachers. In seven schools no record of students' activities of any kind was submitted to parents, and in almost half the schools heads stated that a pupil's non-participation in activities would generally not receive comment in the school report to parents.

Information for the above records was usually obtained through the direct questioning of pupils by the form teacher, although in about a fifth of the schools house-staff had this responsibility, and in two schools those staff responsible for an activity supplied lists of regular participants to the form tutors. Several heads expressed dissatisfaction with the lack of rigour and efficacy of recording techniques in their schools. It was not an aim of the research at this stage to assess whether certain forms of publicity or certain methods of organization were more effective than others in stimulating a high level of pupil participation. Current practice in 31 comprehensive schools has been described, however, in the belief that it may provide a useful basis for thinking and policy-making in this area of extra-curricular activity.

## Pupil participation in extra-curricular activities

The main purpose of the survey of voluntary extra-curricular activities was to assess the degree to which boys and girls of differing year-groups, abilities and social classes took part and, complementarily, to obtain some measure of the extent of non-involvement.

Degree of involvement in activities was assessed by the number of clubs, societies, groups or teams to which a pupil belonged. Pupils recorded this, together with other particulars about their activities, on a short questionnaire. On average, these were received from 87 per cent of the pupils in each school taking part, and data from them were analysed for an average of 84 per cent of each school's pupils.[1] From this information, we were able to compare the participation of different groups of pupils using three measures:

1. the proportion of pupils in each group who took no part in any activity;

2. the proportion of pupils who were relatively well-involved in activities, defined as those pupils taking part in two or more activities;

3. the mean number of activities per pupil.

These measures can only give a rough indication of involvement. The number of a pupil's activities does not, for example, indicate a pupil's role in any club or society, nor does it enable inferences to be made about time-commitment, which would vary according to the nature of the activities pursued.

[1] Approximately three per cent of the questionnaires returned could not be used, generally because no information on the pupils completing them appeared on the pupil data lists sent by schools.

## Voluntary Extra-Curricular Activities

The participation of some 15,500 pupils in 17 schools was studied. Twelve of these schools were mixed with an age-range of pupils from 11-18 years, three were girls' single-sex schools and the remaining two junior and senior high schools respectively.

### The general level of participation

Schools varied considerably in their level of pupil participation, with the average number of activities per pupil varying from less than one to over three.

The extent of non-involvement in activities was considered of particular interest and Table 6.1 summarizes the data on this.

TABLE 6.1: *Non-participation in activities*

| | PERCENTAGE OF NON-PARTICIPANTS IN EACH SCHOOL | | | | |
|---|---|---|---|---|---|
| | 29% and Less | 30%-39% | 40%-49% | 50%-59% | 60% and Over |
| Number of Schools (Total 17) | 2 | 6 | 4 | 4 | 1 |

In all except two of the 17 schools, at least 30 per cent of the pupils took no part in any activities and, in one instance, this rose to over 60 per cent. In over half the schools studied this totally uninvolved group included 40 per cent or more of the pupils.

Generally speaking, between 20 and 30 per cent of the pupils took part in one activity only, but the proportions of the more committed pupils varied considerably.

TABLE 6.2: *High participation in activities*

| | PERCENTAGE OF PUPILS WITH TWO OR MORE ACTIVITIES IN EACH SCHOOL | | | | |
|---|---|---|---|---|---|
| | 29% and Less | 30%-39% | 40%-49% | 50%-59% | 60% and Over |
| Number of Schools (Total 17) | 8 | 6 | 1 | 0 | 2 |

141

Table 6.2 shows that pupils taking part in two or more activities formed less than 30 per cent of the population in nearly half the schools, and in only three did this 'high-participant' group include 40 per cent or more.

In the group of 11,203 pupils (5,728 boys and 5,475 girls) in the 12 mixed all-through schools, over 4,000 (38 per cent) took no part in any school clubs, societies or teams; some 2,930 (26 per cent) took part in one activity and 3,980 (36 per cent) took part in two or more activities. The average number of activities per pupil in these mixed schools was 1·37, but the variation was considerable.

## The Participation of Different Year-Groups

Given that the general level of participation varied from school to school, were there patterns of participation common to pupils in various year-groups? To answer this question, the pupils in the 17 schools were considered in four year-groupings: first-year pupils; second- and third-year pupils; fourth- and fifth-year pupils; sixth-form pupils. The above groups were chosen with various questions in mind. Did first-years, for example, initially join clubs with enthusiasm only to withdraw later: alternatively, did participation increase as pupils settled into the school community? The second- and third-year groups were taken together since they had had time to settle and were neither involved with external examinations nor with the immediate prospect of leaving. The fourth- and fifth-years, on the other hand, were generally concerned with either examinations or leaving. The sixth-form pupils were considered as a separate entity so that the extent of their involvement in the wider extra-curricular life of the school could be studied.

The pattern of participation of the different year-groups varied considerably among schools but involvement tended to decrease in the fourth and fifth years and to increase, quite markedly in many instances, in the sixth form (see diagrams 6.1 and 6.2).

Comparing adjacent year-groups in more detail and using non-participation as the measure of comparison, there was a tendency for the proportion of non-participants to increase between the first and the second and third year-groups in 11 of the 16 schools,[1] but this tendency reaches significance in only six schools. The remaining five schools show significantly the reverse trend and, as well as this, in half the schools the proportion of pupils with two or more activities actually increases in the second and third year-groups and in nine of these older pupils average more activities.

[1] The Senior High School is omitted.

142

## Voluntary Extra-Curricular Activities

DIAGRAM 6.1: *Year-group and participation—percentage of non-participants*

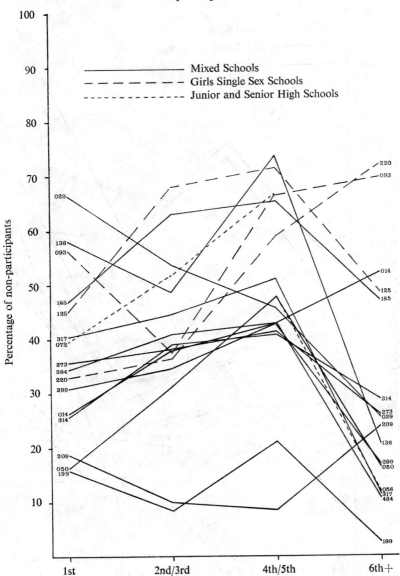

DIAGRAM 6.2: *Year-group and participation—percentage of
high-participants*

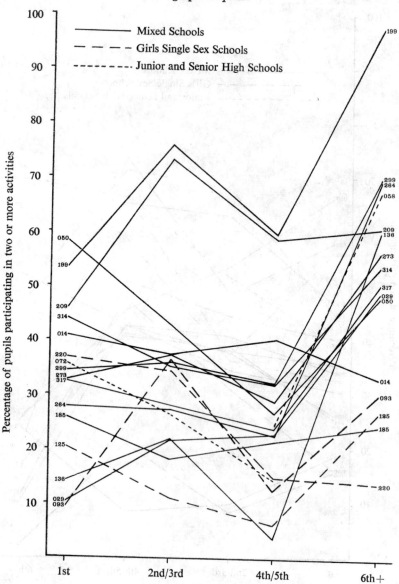

The proportion of totally uninvolved pupils tended to increase in a pronounced way between the second and third and the fourth and fifth years in 14 of the 16 schools (significant in seven), and the reduced level of participation in the older year-group was reflected also in the smaller proportion of pupils taking part in two or more activities (found in 13 schools) and in the decrease in the average number of activities per pupil observable in 12 schools and significant in eight.

In 12 of the 16 schools with sixth-form pupils, there was a lower proportion of non-participants in this year-group than in the fourth- and fifth-year grouping and in all but two schools the sixth-formers averaged more activities per student. Differences between these year-groups were significant in 11 schools on both measures. The proportion of pupils pursuing two or more activities increased markedly among sixth-formers in all but a few schools.

The participation of the 11,203 pupils in the mixed all-through schools divided into year-groups is shown in Table 6.3.

TABLE 6.3: *Year-group and participation (pupils at mixed all-through schools only)*

| Year Groups (N) | ACTIVITIES OF PUPILS | | | Mean Number of Activities |
| | None % | One % | Two or More % | |
|---|---|---|---|---|
| 1st (2319) .. .. | 33 | 30 | 36 | 1·34 |
| 2nd and 3rd (4723) .. | 38 | 25 | 37 | 1·43 |
| 4th and 5th (3457) .. | 45 | 25 | 29 | 1·18 |
| 6th and Over (704) .. | 22 | 22 | 57 | 2·06 |
| *All Years (11,203)* .. | 38 | 26 | 36 | 1·37 |

The reduced level of participation among fourth- and fifth-year pupils and the increased involvement of sixth-formers is clearly seen. Concerning the first of these, we do not know why the tendency to decreased participation in activities occurs at this stage—the demands of external examinations, a preoccupation with leaving school, a lack of interest in the range of activities provided or more broadly in the whole idea of school-centred activities might all be factors. A later section shows that the increased participation of sixth-formers cannot be wholly attributed to the fact that it is the active and more

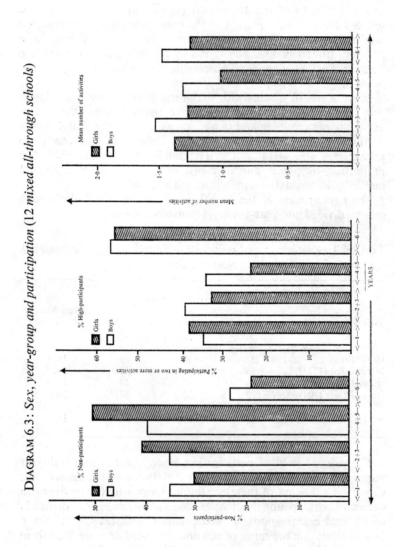

DIAGRAM 6.3: *Sex, year-group and participation (12 mixed all-through schools)*

able who tend to pursue sixth-form courses and other explanations may be relevant. With fewer subjects to study, pupils might have more time for this aspect of school life than previously; the increased specialization of some sixth-form courses might stimulate pupils to widen their interests in extra-curricular activities and schools might be more adept at diagnosing and catering for the activity preferences of this near-adult group than they are for the fourth- and fifth-years. Schools might also tend to encourage sixth-form pupils to take part in, and indeed to initiate and run activities more than they do with the other age-groups. All these, and other factors relating to pupil participation at various stages, merit further attention.

## Differences in the Participation of Boys and Girls

Diagram 6.3 shows the relative participation of the boys and girls in each year-group in the 12 mixed all-through schools. Taking all years together in this mixed-school population, boys were more involved in activities than girls, with highly significant differences between the sexes occurring in the proportions of non-participants, high participants and the average number of activities per pupil. This tendency for boys to take more part in out-of-classroom activities was found in all schools when the mean number of activities was used as a measure of participation (but differences were significant in only five schools), and in 11 schools when the level of participation was assessed by the proportion of non-participant pupils in the two groups (significant in four schools).

Differences between the sexes in the first year were slight and no consistent tendency was found, although the figures for the total population indicate that, overall, the first-year girls were slightly more involved than the boys. At sixth-form level, boys and girls participated to roughly the same degree. In the second and third year-groups and in the fourth and fifth years, the boys as a whole were more active (Diagram 6.3) with differences in each instance reaching a very high level of significance. In individual schools, second- and third-year boys averaged more activities per pupil than the girls in every school (but differences were significant in only six schools) and had proportionately fewer non-participants in nine schools (significantly so in four). Among the older middle-school pupils the boys' superiority is once more reflected on both these measures in all but one of the schools; but the tendency again fails to reach significance in a number of cases (the differences in the proportions of non-participants being significant in seven schools, and between the means in only four). The diagram indicates a difference in the pattern of the participation of the sexes as they progress from the first to the second and third year-groups, where the boys' involvement in activities tends to increase, whereas that of the girls declines. This pattern was found in just over half the schools.

## The Participation of Pupils in Different Ability Groupings

The degree of involvement of pupils of differing levels of ability is of particular interest in a study of comprehensive schools. The schools assigned each pupil a rank on a five-point ability scale, with I being given to the most able pupils and V to the least able. These rankings are particular to each school. Four schools could not provide ability estimates for any of their pupils and a further two gave them for less than 80 per cent of the school population. These were accordingly excluded from this study, leaving 11 schools for which information was virtually complete; these were used in the following analyses.

Table 6.4 shows the proportions of uninvolved and highly involved pupils, for each ability group, and the average number of activities for pupils in each group.

There was a clear general tendency for the percentage of uninvolved pupils to increase as the ability ratings proceed from I to V. The difference in the proportion of uninvolved pupils in Group I as

TABLE 6.4: *Ability and participation*

**Percentage of non-participants**

| ESTIMATED ABILITY | SCHOOLS | | | | | | | | | | |
|---|---|---|---|---|---|---|---|---|---|---|---|
| | 029 | 050 | 185 | 209 | 264 | 314 | 317 | 093 | 125 | 220 | 072 |
| | % | % | % | % | % | % | % | % | % | % | % |
| I | 24 | 26 | 32 | 11 | 25 | 17 | 35 | 43 | 44 | 42 | 25 |
| II | 41 | 28 | 58 | 10 | 36 | 32 | 34 | 30 | 55 | 42 | 41 |
| III | 60 | 33 | 61 | 15 | 41 | 35 | 44 | 53 | 68 | 40 | 49 |
| IV | 73 | 27 | 80 | 12 | 60 | 43 | 52 | 60 | 72 | 46 | 50 |
| V | 82 | 55 | 94 | 20 | 57 | 67 | 76 | 66 | 82 | 60 | 67 |
| *All* | 51 | 33 | 59 | 12 | 37 | 36 | 43 | 53 | 63 | 44 | 50 |
| Significance of $\chi^2$ values | 001 | 001 | 001 | NS | 001 | 001 | 001 | NS | 001 | NS | 01 |

**Percentage of high participants**

| Estimated Ability | Schools | | | | | | | | | | |
|---|---|---|---|---|---|---|---|---|---|---|---|
| | 029 | 050 | 185 | 209 | 264 | 314 | 317 | 093 | 125 | 220 | 072 |
| | % | % | % | % | % | % | % | % | % | % | % |
| I | 42 | 46 | 45 | 68 | 46 | 50 | 38 | 34 | 25 | 28 | 47 |
| II | 28 | 45 | 22 | 62 | 28 | 40 | 35 | 24 | 19 | 29 | 38 |
| III | 14 | 40 | 16 | 62 | 30 | 38 | 30 | 23 | 10 | 29 | 31 |
| IV | 10 | 46 | 2 | 61 | 8 | 33 | 20 | 22 | 8 | 32 | 24 |
| V | 5 | 25 | 0 | 54 | 7 | 12 | 7 | 7 | 3 | 17 | 10 |
| *All* | 22 | 41 | 21 | 62 | 30 | 37 | 30 | 23 | 14 | 30 | 28 |
| Significance of $\chi^2$ values | 001 | 001 | 001 | NS | 001 | 001 | 001 | NS | 001 | NS | 001 |

**Mean number of activities per pupil**

| Estimated Ability | Schools | | | | | | | | | | |
|---|---|---|---|---|---|---|---|---|---|---|---|
| | 029 | 050 | 185 | 209 | 264 | 314 | 317 | 093 | 125 | 220 | 072 |
| I | 1·39 | 1·58 | 1·80 | 2·79 | 1·73 | 2·00 | 1·46 | 1·19 | 0·95 | 1·18 | 1·59 |
| II | 1·07 | 1·83 | 0·91 | 2·34 | 1·15 | 1·40 | 1·31 | 0·82 | 0·72 | 1·12 | 1·27 |
| III | 0·58 | 1·43 | 0·69 | 2·27 | 1·16 | 1·42 | 1·05 | 0·82 | 0·48 | 1·15 | 1·02 |
| IV | 0·42 | 1·70 | 0·23 | 2·18 | 0·51 | 1·19 | 0·84 | 0·73 | 0·40 | 1·08 | 0·97 |
| V | 0·22 | 0·91 | 0·06 | 1·92 | 0·57 | 0·51 | 0·33 | 0·45 | 0·22 | 0·67 | 0·59 |
| *All* | 0·84 | 1·51 | 0·88 | 2·36 | 1·21 | 1·37 | 1·12 | 0·83 | 0·58 | 1·08 | 1·14 |
| Significance of F ratio | 001 | 01 | 001 | 025 | 001 | 001 | 001 | 001 | 001 | 05 | 005 |

compared with Group V is in many cases very considerable—and in the most extreme case (School 185), the lowest ability group has some 62 per cent more non-participants than the highest. In eight schools the differences in the proportions of non-participant pupils in the various ability groupings were highly significant. Of the three schools with non-significant results, in one (School 093), the tendency for a higher proportion of the lower ability pupils to be uninvolved is nevertheless indicated and in School 209, exceptional in its very high level of pupil participation, the lowest ability group again had the highest proportion of non-participants. The third school (220) is interesting because the percentages of uninvolved pupils in the first four ability groupings are much the same, but a difference occurs between these pupils and those in Group V—a pattern also seen in School 050. Both schools had restricted intakes of five per cent or less 'X' or able pupils according to the 1965 estimates and it is thought that differences in ability between the first four ability groups were not large enough to be reflected in differences in participation (see diagram 6.4).

Looking at the distributions of pupils in the various ability groups in the high-participation category, these differed at a very high level of significance from random distributions in eight of the 11 schools— the same schools, in fact, in which non-chance distributions were found for non-participant pupils. In all these schools smaller proportions of the lower ability pupils were involved in two or more activities. This trend is also observable in School 093 and, to a limited extent, in the other two schools where significant results were not obtained (see diagram 6.5).

Table 6.4 gives the mean number of activities per pupil for each ability group and shows that in every school the highest mean occurred in the first two ability groupings and the lowest in Ability Group V. The variations among the means of the ability groups were significant in every school. Significant differences in the mean number of activities occurred most commonly between Groups I and II and between Groups IV and V (eight schools). It may be that schools were able to identify their highest and lowest ability pupils with more accuracy than was possible for the intermediate groups, where distinctions might be difficult to make.

The relationship between participation in activities and ability does not seem to be more pronounced in pupils of either sex, or to increase or decrease as pupils progress through school.

*Ability as an Explanation of Sixth-Form Participation*

Earlier it was shown that sixth-form pupils as a group were more involved in activities than any other year. The relationship between ability and participation might explain this, for the more able are those most likely to pursue sixth-form courses. In other words, the apparent rise in participation may be due simply to the loss of those pupils who did not participate extensively, rather than to any real increase in extra-curricular commitments by pupils when they reach this stage of their school careers.

DIAGRAM 6.4: *Ability and participation—percentage of non-participants*

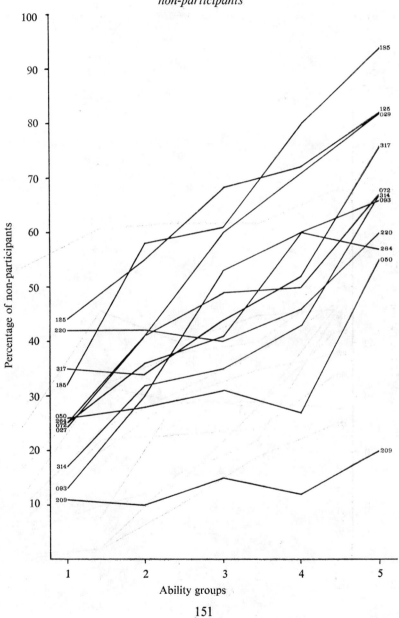

DIAGRAM 6.5: *Ability and participation—percentage of high-participants*

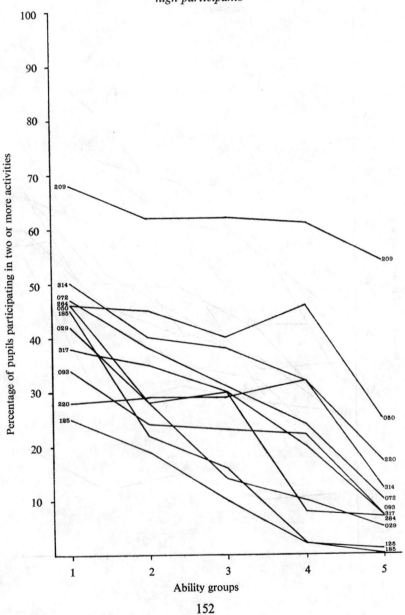

Ten of the 11 schools supplying information on pupils' ability had sixth forms. Table 6.5 shows how sixth-form pupils in these schools were rated for ability.

TABLE 6.5: *The estimated ability of sixth-form pupils*

| | | ABILITY GROUPS | | | | |
|---|---|---|---|---|---|---|
| *School* | *I* | *II* | *III* | *IV* | *V* | *Total* |
| 029 | 29 | 16 | 2 | 0 | 0 | 47 |
| 050 | 29 | 15 | 11 | 0 | 0 | 55 |
| 185 | 26 | 28 | 1 | 0 | 0 | 55 |
| 209 | 17 | 26 | 3 | 0 | 0 | 46 |
| 264 | 41 | 16 | 19 | 0 | 0 | 76 |
| 314 | 18 | 23 | 11 | 0 | 0 | 52 |
| 317 | 30 | 37 | 5 | 0 | 0 | 72 |
| 093 | 7 | 8 | 6 | 6 | 6 | 33 |
| 125 | 75 | 43 | 27 | 5 | 1 | 151 |
| 220 | 22 | 17 | 9 | 2 | 0 | 50 |

Only three schools had any sixth-form pupils assigned to Ability Groups IV and V. To ascertain whether sixth-formers actually took part in more activities than other year-groups, or whether their participation merely reflected the fact that the lower ability pupils had left, comparison was made between the first three ability groupings in the sixth form (which, in all but a few instances, accounts for all sixth-formers) and the first three ability groups in years one to five in each school. The mean number of activities was used as the measure of participation.

Table 6.6 shows that when such a comparison was made, sixth-form pupils still averaged more activities in seven out of the 10 schools and in four the differences were highly significant. The higher ability, then, of sixth-form pupils might account for some of the differences in participation between these pupils and those in other year-groups, but not for all of it. Other factors as well as ability must be sought to explain these pupils' generally higher level of participation. A longitudinal approach might be valuable here.

One of the main goals of the comprehensive school must be to assimilate a varied intake of pupils into as many aspects of school life as possible. School clubs and societies, unencumbered by the demands and divisions which beset much curricular work, afford a

TABLE 6.6: *Participation of sixth-formers compared with pupils in years 1–5*

MEAN NUMBER OF ACTIVITIES

| School | Sixth Form | Years 1–5 | Value of t | p |
|--------|------------|-----------|------------|-----|
| 029 | 1·55 | 0·92 | 3·01 | 0·01 |
| 050 | 1·93 | 1·57 | 1·62 | NS |
| 185 | 0·93 | 1·19 | 1·47 | NS |
| 209 | 2·39 | 2·45 | <1 | NS |
| 264 | 2·38 | 1·15 | 6·62 | 0·001 |
| 314 | 1·85 | 1·62 | <1 | NS |
| 317 | 1·92 | 1·19 | 4·60 | 0·001 |
| 093 | 0·95 | 0·90 | <1 | NS |
| 125 | 1·03 | 0·61 | 3·71 | 0·001 |
| 220 | 0·78 | 1·18 | 1·51 | NS |

special opportunity of achieving this with regard to pupils of differing abilities, and it seems desirable that the least able as well as the most able pupils should avail themselves of the opportunities they offer.

The data from the schools show, however, that pupils assessed as more able participate in activities more extensively than the less able. The extent of this relationship between a high ability-rating and a high level of involvement in clubs and societies varies but it was present in all the 11 schools used in this part of the research, and in every school significant differences between the ability groups were found on at least one measure of participation.

At this stage the factors contributing or related to the lower level of involvement of the less able have not been examined. Analyses are, however, in progress which will indicate whether the lower ability groups tend to find their interests less adequately catered for than their counterparts in the higher ability categories. Data for a study of pupils' activity preferences have also been collected, and the analysis of those should throw some light on the problem of identifying activities most likely to attract the interest and co-operation of the less able.

Finally, involvement in activities is perhaps most satisfactorily regarded as part of a pupil's total involvement in the school community. Less able pupils may be generally less school-centred and low participation in school activities may be merely a reflection of this fact. This suggestion receives support from the later finding that those pupils least committed to activities are also those who spend least time on homework. If this indicates 'academic commitment' to the school, then pupils least involved in the voluntary aspects of school life are also those least committed academically. It must be remembered, too, that the ability rating was a school assessment and thus likely itself to be a measure of academic commitment. Future studies might usefully examine the participation of the less able pupils in terms of their total involvement in, and satisfaction with, the school community in all its aspects.

*The Participation of Pupils in Different Social Classes*

Schools detailed the parental (i.e. fathers') occupations of their pupils and these were classified in accordance with the five groupings of the Registrar-General's social class scale (1966).[1] Some schools had difficulty in providing this information and, as a result, this study of participation and social class could be conducted in only 13 of the 17 schools. In these, the majority, although not all pupils, could be classified.

Eight of the schools studied in this section were mixed all-through schools, four rurally situated and four in urban areas. As it was considered likely that the nature and effect of the social structure of a rural as opposed to an urban area would differ, the schools, as well as being studied individually, were compared in these two groups. The three girls' single-sex schools and the junior and senior high schools also provided satisfactory information on the parental occupations of their pupils and these schools, too, are included in this study.

1. *The rural schools.* All four rural schools had comparatively high proportions of pupils classifiable in social classes I and II and very few, by contrast, in social class V.[2] The first point may be explained by the large number of farmers' children in these schools (farmers, farm managers and market gardeners, with or without employees and regardless of size of holding, are all in this scale classified in social class II) and the second by the fact that Group V (unskilled) occupations tend to be more commonly found in urban areas.[3]

[1] The social classes I to V are outlined in Appendix C.

[2] We were able to classify some 75 per cent of the total population of these schools from the parental occupation data received.

[3] E.g. porter, sweeper, cleaner, ticket collector, kitchen hand, dock labourer, stevedore, messenger, guard.

In only one rural school were significant differences found among the parental occupation groupings on any of the measures of participation, and here pupils in the higher social classifications took part in more activities than those allocated to social classes IV and V. In one other rural school, a greater proportion of pupils in social classes I and II than IV and V took part in two or more activities— but differences were not significant on this or other measures of participation. In neither of the other two rural schools was there any evidence of a relationship between involvement and social class.

When the pupils in the four rural schools are regarded as a single population, certain participation patterns emerge for the different social groups (Table 6.7).

TABLE 6.7: *Social class and participation—4 rural schools*

| Social Class | None % | One % | Two or more % | N | All % | Mean Number of Activities |
|---|---|---|---|---|---|---|
| | | | | | | |
| I and II | 24 | 23 | 53 | 698 | 100 | 2·16 |
| III | 27 | 23 | 51 | 560 | 100 | 2·09 |
| IV | 31 | 22 | 47 | 332 | 100 | 2·03 |
| V | 29 | 22 | 49 | 41 | 100 | 1·92 |
| All | 27 | 23 | 51 | 1631 | 100 | 2·10 |
| Significance Level of $\chi^2$ Values | NS | NS | NS | — | — | F<1 NS |

*Note:* For the purposes of the chi-square test, social classes I and II and IV and V were combined both in the analyses for individual schools and in those for the total rural and urban school population.

Table 6.7 shows that 24 per cent of pupils in social classes I and II took no part at all in activities as compared with 31 per cent of pupils in classes IV and V combined. Complementarily, 53 per cent of the first two social classes were high participants compared with 47 per cent of pupils in classes IV and V. These differences, however, did not achieve significance and neither did the variation among the means shown on the table, although, again, the means tend to decrease with social class.

156

2. *The urban schools.* Again, in only one of the four mixed all-through schools were differences in participation among the social groups significant on one or more of the measures. Unlike the rural schools, however, in those three schools where differences were not significant, the higher social groups revealed a greater tendency to take part in activities. In all three schools, classes I and II had a lower proportion of pupils completely uninvolved than was the case among class V pupils, and in each school the mean number of activities per pupil decreased as the social class scale was descended.

Table 6.8 shows the participation of pupils in the different social classes in these four urban-situated schools, treated as a single population.

TABLE 6.8: *Social class and participation—4 urban schools*

| | ACTIVITIES OF PUPILS | | | | | |
| Social Class | None | One | Two or more | All | | Mean Number of Activities |
| | % | % | % | N | % | |
| I and II | 36 | 27 | 37 | 266 | 100 | 1·35 |
| III | 46 | 25 | 29 | 2233 | 100 | 1·09 |
| IV | 46 | 27 | 27 | 527 | 100 | 1·07 |
| V | 55 | 23 | 22 | 420 | 100 | 0·88 |
| *All* | 46 | 25 | 29 | 3446 | 100 | 1·08 |
| Significance Level of $\chi^2$ Values | 01 | NS | 001 | — | — | F=6·25 p<0·001 |

Once the urban population is taken as a whole, highly significant differences in the participation of the social classes appear on all measures. This may be compared with our findings for the total rural school population (Table 6.7).

Five schools in addition to those above provided us with the opportunity of studying participation in relation to social class. Three of these were girls' single-sex schools in urban areas. In only one of these did the pupils in the higher social groupings participate more extensively, and here significant differences were found on all measures of participation.

Significant participation differences were again found in the one senior high school in this study, with pupils in the top two social classes showing a higher level of involvement. In the junior high school, most of the pupils were classified in social classes III and IV and the former group showed the higher level of participation. Differences among the social groups, however, were not significant on any of the measures in this school.

The relationship between participation in activities and social class, as measured by parental occupation, appears to be neither as marked, nor as universal, as that between participation and ability. To look at this more closely, a study was made of the effect of both variables simultaneously in five schools where the quality of pupil information supplied on both ability and parental occupation made this possible. The mean number of activities of pupils in each ability grouping within each social class are shown in Appendix Table A6.1 and the results of the analyses of variance appear in Table 6.9. This gives the results in each school of analysis of the variation among the means for all ability groups and all social classes; the means for the social classes within the ability groups; and the means for the five ability groups.

TABLE 6.9: *Social class, ability and participation—analysis of variance (significance levels)*

| SCHOOL | VARIATION AMONG MEANS FOR ALL ABILITY AND ALL SOCIAL GROUPS | | VARIATION AMONG MEANS FOR SOCIAL CLASSES WITHIN ABILITY GROUPS | | VARIATION AMONG MEANS FOR ABILITY GROUPS | |
|---|---|---|---|---|---|---|
| | F-Ratio | p | F-Ratio | p | F-Ratio | p |
| 125 | 4·24 | 001 | 1·32 | NS | 15·17 | 001 |
| 185 | 5·39 | 001 | 5·98 | 001 | 28·96 | 001 |
| 209 | 1·05 | NS | <1 | NS | 1·98 | NS* |
| 314 | 6·36 | 001 | <1 | NS | 27·39 | 001 |
| 317 | 3·66 | 001 | 1·48 | NS | 11·87 | 001 |

*$p < 0.1$

The differences among the means for all ability and social classifications were very highly significant in four of the five schools. But in only one school were variations among the means for the social classes within the ability groups significantly non-chance. The final columns of Table 6.9 show the variations between ability groups to be by contrast very highly significant in all but one school and significant at the 10 per cent level in School 209 (where the overall variations had not achieved significance). Comparison of the size of the F-ratios found in the between-ability group analysis with those in the first column shows the variation between ability groups to be the most important contributing factor to the total variance.

To summarize, indications of a tendency for participation in activities to decrease as the social class scale is descended were discernible in nine out of the 13 schools which provided parental occupation information. The strength of this tendency, however, varied greatly from school to school and in only four schools were differences in the participation of the social classes statistically significant on one or more of the participation measures. It appears from our data that the degree of relationship between parental occupation and participation might vary according to the location of the school. There was considerably less evidence of the relationship in rural schools compared with urban schools. It should be noted, however, that the classification scale used may not adequately discriminate cultural, economic and aspirational differences among certain rural occupations which are likely to affect a pupil's participation. Finally, the tendency for higher social classification to be associated with high participation was generally neither as marked, nor as universal as that noted for high ability-rating.

### Environmental factors and participation in extra-curricular activities

The previous sections have examined the relationship between certain pupil variables—year-group, sex, ability and social class—and participation in school-run activities. It seemed likely, however, that other factors might influence the extent of a pupil's involvement in these. We considered here, for example, other demands on a pupil's time—time needed for travelling, for homework and for activities unconnected with school. Also, some schools might have only limited facilities and offer a restricted range of extra-curricular activities. Parental attitudes to such activities might also be important and there might be pressures on some pupils to take paid jobs after school rather than stay for school clubs and societies. This section studies these factors, using data from the pupils' questionnaires in those 17 schools where an intensive study was made, and from the interviews with the heads of the 31 which provided the information for the first part of this chapter.

159

From the heads' assessments it appeared that after-school employment or domestic commitments, membership of non-school activities
and unsympathetic parental attitudes deterred a sizeable proportion
of pupils from taking part in clubs and societies in fewer than one-
third of the 31 schools. All but one of the seven schools in which
the head considered that jobs and other four o'clock commitments
impaired participation were located in less prosperous urban areas.
The majority of heads interviewed felt that local activities offered
little threat to those in their schools, and several made the point that
those pupils most active in local clubs and societies were also those
most involved at school. Belonging to youth clubs or farming or
village activities were thought to impair participation in only nine
schools.

Parental attitudes may act as important determinants of participation in school activities, and in eight schools the heads considered
adverse pressure at home to be a problem; over half of the heads said
that they met unsympathetic attitudes towards extra-curricular work
fairly often. Most commonly, these arose from anxiety over the
pupil's later return from school. To counteract this, one school
issued weekly circulars to inform parents of forthcoming events
and one-third of the schools, as previously recorded, ensured that
parents were informed of pupils' extra-curricular commitments by
detailing these fully on the school report. Parents were seldom
regularly involved, either as organizers or participants in school
activities, although frequently their financial contributions provided
a valued stimulus to this part of a school's work.

Another factor affecting participation was the duration of a pupil's
journey home; in rural schools, pupils with long journeys (i.e. 45
minutes and over) generally took part in fewer activities. This
tendency was found in three of the four rural schools where an
intensive study of pupil participation was made, and reached
significance in two schools. The fourth rural school concentrated its
activities in an extended lunch-hour and so is not relevant to this
discussion. In nine of the 13 urban schools, by contrast, pupils with
long journeys were frequently those most involved in activities and
differences here reached significance in four schools. A possible
explanation of this suggested by evidence from one school is that
pupils with long journeys in these schools may be those of higher
ability recruited from outside the school's immediate neighbourhood.
Further analysis of the data would be necessary before such an
explanation could be generally applied, and other possibilities should
not be overlooked: pupils travelling long distances may tend to make

160

school the centre of their social and cultural activities, since they have less time for involvement with peers and for activities in their own home neighbourhoods.

The intensive study of participation in the 17 schools showed that relatively heavy homework assignments did not prevent pupils from taking part in activities—in fact, the data show convincingly that those pupils spending most time on homework were those most involved in clubs and societies. A high level of 'academic commitment' —if time spent on homework can be taken as an indication of this— is, on the whole, accompanied by a high level of 'social involvement' as measured by participation in activities. In 12 of the 17 schools participation increased with the amount of time spent on homework and the variations among the means for the different time-groups achieved a high level of significance. In a further four, indications of the same tendency were found. In one school only was there no evidence of such a relationship. Diagram 6.6 presents the data for the 12 mixed all-through schools, regarded as a single population. The histograms show clearly that, as time spent on homework increases, so also does extra-curricular participation.

As pupils progress through school, homework demands generally become heavier. The study of pupils in different year-groups showed that involvement in activities decreased among fourth- and fifth-year pupils and it was suggested that this might be explained in terms of heavier 'academic' demands. Table 6.10 gives the mean number of activities of pupils spending different lengths of time on homework in each year-group in the total population of the 12 mixed all-through schools.

TABLE 6.10: *Homework time and participation: mean number of activities*

| YEAR-GROUP | HOMEWORK TIME | | | | | | | F-RATIO | p |
|---|---|---|---|---|---|---|---|---|---|
| | 15 Mins. and Less | 30 Mins. | 45 Mins. | 1 Hour | 1½ Hours | 2½ Hours | All | | |
| 1st .. .. | 1·24 | 1·25 | 1·35 | 1·37 | 1·63 | 1·64 | 1·34 | 3·97 | 005 |
| 2nd & 3rd .. | 1·04 | 1·26 | 1·38 | 1·57 | 1·82 | 1·93 | 1·43 | 27·22 | 001 |
| 4th & 5th .. | 0·68 | 0·80 | 1·00 | 1·16 | 1·41 | 1·78 | 1·18 | 49·15 | 001 |
| 6th & over .. | 1·32 | 1·03 | 1·97 | 1·88 | 1·93 | 2·29 | 2·05 | 5·06 | 001 |
| *All* .. .. | 0·95 | 1·16 | 1·30 | 1·43 | 1·65 | 1·92 | 1·37 | 80·75 | 001 |

161

F

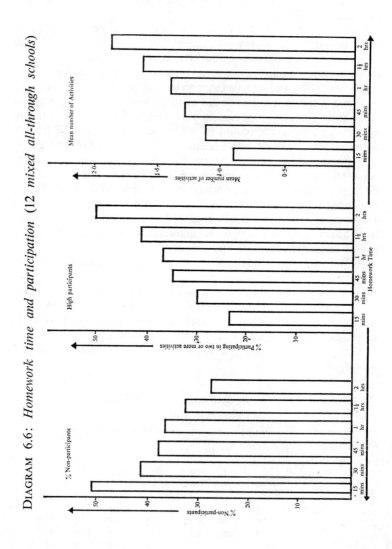

DIAGRAM 6.6: *Homework time and participation (12 mixed all-through schools)*

In each year-group the pupils spending more time on homework are those who take part in more activities, and the table shows that homework commitments cannot be used to explain reduced participation in any year-group and certainly not in the fourth and fifth year.

It seems probable that ability accounts for these findings—the pupils giving more time to homework are likely to be those of higher ability and a strong relationship has been found between ability and participation. This explanation is supported by the fact that in four of the five schools where differences in participation between the various homework time groups were not significant, the relationship between ability and participation was comparatively weak.

## The Contribution of Teaching Staff

Over two-thirds of the heads in their general comments on factors determining the level of pupil participation in their schools considered the contributions made by teaching staff to be crucial. Given that in most schools activities are mainly teacher-initiated and organized, the extent to which staff feel inclined and are able to provide a variety of activities must largely determine the pupils' opportunities for extra-curricular participation. The heads of nearly half of the 31 schools considered the general level of activity in their schools to be limited by the extent of the staff contribution, and several drew attention to the particular difficulties of married female staff in undertaking additional commitments after school. The staff contribution can be assessed by considering the proportion of teachers involved in activities and the amount of time they give to them, and two sources provide evidence which is relevant here. First, Monks (1968), reporting on the 331 schools in the first survey, found that 60 per cent of all teachers in these schools took part in extra-curricular activities, but that a higher proportion of men than women were involved in this way (66 per cent as compared with 49 per cent). Second, in connection with this present study, a survey was made of 431 teachers who organized or took part in the main activities in their schools, in order to find out what this meant in terms of extra time-commitments. We found that on average these teachers spent some two and three-quarter hours each week on this extra work, while some 40 per cent gave three hours or more, and over 25 per cent four hours or more. The average weekly time for married and single male and female staff in this group is detailed in Table 6.11.

This shows that the men as a group gave more time to activities than the women, with the difference between the sexes reaching a very high level of significance. More time also was spent by single than married staff, although only in the case of single as compared with married men were differences significant. The most involved group, then (in terms of time-commitment) was the single men, who averaged 3·4 hours per week on extra-curricular activities, and the least involved, the married women (2·1 hours). The lower level of involvement of women generally might partly explain the low level of pupil participation found in the three girls' single-sex schools in the study, and also the lower participation of the girls in the mixed schools.

TABLE 6.11: *Hours per week spent on activities by participant staff according to sex and marital status*

|  |  |  |  | MARRIED | SINGLE | BOTH |
|---|---|---|---|---|---|---|
| Men | .. | .. | .. | 2·9 | 3·4 | 3·0 |
| (N) | .. | .. | .. | (204) | (67) | (271) |
| Women | .. | .. | .. | 2·1 | 2·6 | 2·4 |
| (N) | .. | .. | .. | (66) | (94) | (160) |
| Both | .. | .. | .. | 2·7 | 2·9 | 2·8 |
| (N) | .. | .. | .. | (270) | (161) | (431) |

Since the willingness and ability of staff to run activities is clearly of importance, the incentives offered to teachers undertaking these might bear further consideration and investigation. In only three of our 31 schools were compensatory free periods given to staff with heavy extra-curricular commitments and although, as reported earlier, heads were almost wholly agreed as to the importance of the extra-curricular aspect of school provision, over two-thirds did not regard the ability and willingness to take part in activities as constituting a criterion for appointing staff. In those eight schools where the heads did have this criterion, its operation was frequently impeded by shortage of candidates. It appears that only rarely will a teacher be appointed for his possible contribution to the extra-curricular as well as the curricular life of a school. Heads were generally anxious that staff participation in clubs and societies should remain voluntary—

although this did not apply to activities connected with certain curricular subjects, such as physical education, music and English (drama), where their provision was expected 'as a matter of course'. In only three schools did heads expect activities to be run as a matter of routine by subject departments in addition to those mentioned above.

Staff and pupil participation alike may be influenced by the nature of the school buildings and the facilities available. In two-thirds of the schools heads described these as generally satisfactory but the remainder considered their schools to be handicapped in this respect. In these, absence of the right kind of space and/or difficulties in communication were thought to deter staff and pupils from undertaking extra-curricular pursuits.

The discussion above has shown that the extent of the teaching staff's contribution was thought to be an important determinant of the level of pupil participation in most schools. Many of the other factors studied, however—after-school employment, non-school activities, length of journey home, parental attitudes, the adequacy of school buildings and facilities—were found to vary in their influence from one geographical area to another, from school to school and from pupil to pupil. A finding of interest in this section was that heavy homework commitments did not, as might have been expected, deter pupils from undertaking extra-curricular commitments; the pupils who were more involved in activities were those spending a greater amount of time on homework.

Much of the information on which this section is based is 'indirect' in that it relies on the observations of the heads. Future research might profitably carry out a more detailed investigation of some of the above factors and their interrelationships, using material collected directly from the pupils themselves.

## Summary

A study of school policy towards voluntary extra-curricular activities and of factors considered likely to affect pupil participation was made in 31 schools. In 17 of these a detailed analysis of participation was made in terms of pupils' year-group, sex, estimated ability and social class. The main findings are summarized below.

### Policy, Organization and Publicity

1. The heads were in almost complete agreement as to the value of extra-curricular activities. Most frequently they saw them as a means

of achieving social cohesiveness in a school, of fostering staff-student relationships, of educating pupils for leisure, of supplementing curricular instruction and of providing pursuits not in the normal curriculum.

2. Nearly two-thirds of the schools adhered to a 'traditional' pattern of holding activities in a lunch hour of normal duration and after school; interesting deviations most frequently found in rural schools were extended lunch hours, and the allocation of curricular time for these pursuits. A few schools provided evening youth clubs run exclusively for pupils by members of the school staff.

3. In organizing these activities, the most common practice was for some to be run on a whole-school basis and some to be centred around sections of it. The smaller schools tended to organize all their activities on a whole-school basis, but the larger, by contrast, used only school divisions. Few schools used the house system to operate a continuous and varied extra-curricular programme.

4. Activities were mainly teacher-initiated and organized. In very few schools did the pupils supply the initiative for most of the activities, and only one example of an activity which was run wholly by the pupils was found.

5. In addition to the normal publicity via notice-board and assembly announcements, a few schools issued regular circulars to pupils and, in one instance, to parents, providing information on forthcoming events. Similarly, some schools had interesting ways of bringing activity 'achievements' to the notice of their pupils—the production of regular bulletins with accounts of activity meetings; providing 'unattached' pupils with the opportunity to see clubs and societies in action; and five schools pursued a policy of getting local press coverage for as much of the school's activity as possible.

6. Heads were seldom personally involved in clubs and societies, although they acted in most cases as co-ordinators of the extra-curricular programme. Commonly they visited activities, but few set aside time specifically for this and as many as nine of the 31 interviewed made such visits rarely, if at all.

7. Pupil participation was recorded on the record card, school report to parents or the testimonial in all but four schools. Whereas most schools detailed a pupil's activities on his record card, in only one-third were these fully specified on the reports to parents. Schools were divided almost equally as regards the inclusion on reports of comments on non-participation in activities.

*Pupil Participation*

8. In all but two schools, over one-third of the pupils were not involved in any activities. Usually, about one-quarter took part in one activity. Pupils more highly committed frequently accounted for less than 30 per cent of the school's population, and rarely exceeded 40 per cent.

9. The level of participation fell among pupils in the later middle-school year-group (i.e. in the fourth and fifth years). In the sixth form, by contrast, the level of participation usually showed a marked rise.

10. Girls were less involved in activities than boys in the middle-school years; there was little difference in participation between the sexes in the first and the sixth forms.

11. Pupils of higher estimated ability were more involved in activities than their less able counterparts in all schools. The apparent rise in the level of involvement of sixth-form pupils may be partially (but not wholly) explained by the dropping out of the less able pupils at this stage.

12. A tendency was also found for participation in activities to decrease among pupils from the less skilled occupation groups. Generally, this was not marked, and significant differences in participation among the social classes occurred in four schools only.

13. Our findings suggest a need to discover ways of integrating the less able pupils and the other low participant groups discussed above into the extra-curricular aspects of school life. Further research might seek to help teachers in their extra-curricular work by examining the attitudes which accompany the limited involvement of these groups, and identifying activities most likely to attract those pupils who at present tend to be minimally involved.

*Factors Affecting Participation*

14. After-school employment, membership of activities unconnected with school and unsympathetic parental attitudes towards activities were estimated to deter a sizeable proportion of pupils from participating in fewer than one-third of the schools.

15. Over half the heads, however, said they frequently encountered unfavourable parental attitudes, arising most commonly from anxiety over a pupil's later return home. Parents were fully informed of pupils' activities in only one-third of the schools, and were themselves rarely involved in this part of the school's work, either as organizers or participants.

16. Pupils in rural schools with long journeys generally took part in fewer activities. In urban schools, by contrast, pupils with long journeys were frequently those most involved.

17. Spending a long time on homework did not prevent pupils from taking part in activities. Those pupils spending least time on homework were also those least involved in clubs and societies; level of 'academic involvement' and of 'social involvement' were closely related.

18. The contribution made by the teaching staff was considered by the heads to be a major factor determining the general level of participation in the majority of schools—this follows from our finding that activities are mainly teacher-initiated and organized.

19. Generally, the time commitment for teachers involved in activities was considerable; on average, staff organizing or participating in activities spent about two and three-quarter hours each week on this additional work.

20. Women staff were less involved in activities than men.

21. Rarely was compensatory free time given to staff with heavy extra-curricular commitments, and the appointment of staff to schools for their possible contribution to extra-curricular as well curricular life was also rare.

22. Generally, the provision of activities was expected as a matter of course only from physical education, music and English (drama) departments. In only three schools did heads expect activities to be organized as a matter of routine by departments in addition to those mentioned above. The relationship between the 'voluntariness' of staff-involvement in this aspect of the school's work, on the one hand, and the needs of the pupils on the other, was generally undefined.

# CHAPTER SEVEN

# Contacts Between the School and the Community

*by* T. KAWWA *and* T. S. ROBERTSON

JUST as primary schools are there to educate the children of the neighbourhood, so comprehensive schools may aim to serve all boys and girls in their area and be an integral part of the life of the local community. Ideally, the school should reflect the life of the neighbourhood it serves and contribute to it. The greater the links between the two and the more one is part of the other, the greater one may assume the benefit to both.

There is, however, another aspect, for pupils whose parents take an interest in their children's school work and visit the schools make better progress at school and are likely to stay at school longer than children of uninterested and unco-operative parents. The problem confronting the schools is to try and make contact with all parents, so that education is a joint effort between the home and the school. The Plowden Report (1967) stressed the importance of such links, and the operational research work of Young and McGeeney (1968) would seem a promising field of study.

Involvement of the school with the community was briefly studied at the first stage of this research project (Monks, 1968). This chapter looks at this involvement in more detail. Forty-seven heads completed a questionnaire concerned with local contacts which had been shown, by preliminary inquiries to the schools, to be common.

### School functions and activities

All schools conducted activities to which parents, and often members of the public, were invited. Athletic events, musical or theatrical performances, open days, exhibitions of pupils' work, social or party evenings, fêtes and careers conventions were each found in the majority of schools. Although the age-range of the pupils in the school and its catchment area did not seem to be linked with occurrence or frequency of these events, the Midlands and South had more regular school activities than the North, with

169

Welsh schools having the least. This was reflected in the greater variety of activities given financial support by parents in the Midlands and South. New schools, and adapted schools with grammar schools in their origin, tended to have more social and musical evenings and theatrical performances than did the other adapted schools (see Appendix Table A7.1). The heads of most schools considered the response of both parents and the public to invitations to these functions to be good, or at least satisfactory. The heads of 10 schools, however, considered the general response to be poor or very poor—in one of these, in a remote area, the transport difficulties were considered responsible; the other nine, however, were urban schools.

### Parent-teacher associations

Of the 47 schools, 29 had Parent-Teacher Associations of which 23 had formal constitutions, but only six were affiliated to the National Federation of Parent-Teacher Associations. The commonest activities of the associations were fund-raising ones, such as fêtes and social evenings, but discussions and lectures, including demonstrations of teaching techniques and methods, were frequent. Meetings to discuss the work and prospects of individual pupils were, of course, a prominent feature of parents' meetings. However, in 20 of the 29 schools, parental attendance was reported to be poor, at least for some functions; lack of parental interest and transport difficulties were largely to blame. Thirteen heads said teacher attendance was poor, and this was put down to the long distances many had to travel and the consequent transport problems.

In 12 of the remaining 18 schools without an association the head considered other forms of contact with parents, such as house evenings, to be adequate. Nevertheless, lack of parental co-operation had been responsible for the discontinuance of two associations, as well as for the failure of an attempt to start one in another school. Parent-teacher associations appeared to have the best chance of flourishing in senior high schools and, to a lesser extent, in all-through schools; in junior high schools, on the other hand, parental support for these associations appeared to be less adequate.

### Relationships with former pupils

Every head spoke of visits from former pupils. Sometimes advice was sought but more frequently the call was to meet teachers and old friends. It seems from the answers to the questionnaires that in any one year an average of 63 visits per 1,000 pupils on the roll were made (see Appendix Table A7.2).

Formal old scholars' associations were most common in the former grammar schools, and least common in the former secondary modern schools, but the estimated number of visits by former pupils in the current academic year did not differ significantly between schools of different types.

## School magazines and other publications

Potentially, school magazines are an effective means of bringing the activities of the school to the notice of members of the local community. Thirty-six of the 47 schools had such publications, of which two-thirds were said to be fairly widely distributed. To check this, the number of copies printed for each school was compared with the number of pupils; in seven schools for which information was available, the distribution considerably exceeded the number of pupils; in nine the circulation approximated to the number of pupils, but in 13 schools the number of pupils was greater than the number of copies. It can probably safely be assumed that where there was at least one copy per pupil, the publication was reaching the neighbouring community. A few schools used the school magazine for publicity purposes, for example a school of 550 pupils circulated 3,500 copies of the school magazine, but so large a circulation was exceptional (see Appendix Table A7.3).

## Relationships with other schools and educational organizations

Schools have many links with other communities through co-operation and competition with neighbouring and more distant schools. In these, teachers and pupils may be equally involved. In the transfer of pupils from primary to secondary school, or from junior high school to senior high school, co-operation between schools and the exchange of information about pupils are the rule. Except in the most isolated districts, there is also competition between schools in sport, and co-operation for events such as school journeys, social service, sixth-form discussion groups, religious organizations, music and theatrical activities. Single-sex schools, particularly those for girls, seemed more active in these wider links than mixed schools.

Staff have some contact with those at other schools in their exchange of ideas about curricula, in co-ordinating their curricula, combining school activities, operating CSE examinations and, to quote one responder, 'in the pursuit of common professional interests'.

All the schools that were studied organized educational visits. Most did this regularly as a school policy, but others as and when individual teachers chose to arrange them (see Appendix Table A7.4). Examples of places visited were theatres, art galleries, museums, exhibitions, places of historical and aesthetic interest, hospitals, schools and universities. In the course of a school year an average of 41 per cent of all pupils at the schools studied went for at least one outside visit, but the actual percentage varied from three per cent in one school to 100 per cent in others (see Appendix Table A7.5). Proportionately more pupils were sent out on educational visits in the South and Midlands than in the North and Wales. Educational visits were more frequent in the former secondary modern schools than in former grammar schools. They were also commoner in girls' schools than in mixed schools and in mixed schools than in boys' schools.

Most schools received visits from representatives of external bodies, (e.g. police officers, in connection with road safety, artists and doctors). This kind of visit was most frequent in all-through schools and least common in junior high schools. London schools received most visits, rural schools least.

One important link with higher education is the acceptance each year of student teachers from colleges of education and university departments of education for teaching practice. Each school on average received students from four colleges or departments each year; but schools in the South, and particularly in the London area, received students from more colleges and universities than those elsewhere. Outside the ILEA area urban and rural schools differed little, but the Welsh ones were in contact with a few colleges only. Contacts with British or foreign academic institutions were mentioned by roughly half the heads, and 38 of the 47 schools had received visits from foreign educationists in the last two years.

**Visits to factories, farms and commercial firms**

In addition to the educational and cultural visits, there were many vocational visits. Thirty-six of the 47 schools regularly organized this kind of visit as a matter of school policy (see Appendix Table A7.4). An average of 22 per cent of pupils on the school roll made vocational visits in the year, the proportion being larger in small than large schools (see Appendix Table A7.5). Ten schools had pupils on day release to firms, the number of pupils varying from 20 to 300.

## Voluntary social work by staff

An unofficial, but important link between school and community can be the performance of voluntary social work by members of the staff. In over half the schools, it was known that such voluntary social work was undertaken, but this was probably an understatement of the actual number.

## Non-teaching staff

In addition to the pupils and teaching staff, a considerable number of workers are employed at a school and to a greater or lesser extent are identified with it. These are the non-teaching staff, including cleaners, school meals staff, caretakers, groundsmen, laboratory and secretarial staff. The average number of people employed in this way was 29 non-teaching staff to each school. All these are likely to convey some impression of the school to the community it serves, and so help to forge links between the school and the community.

## School courses of study on community relationship

The contacts with the community discussed so far have been of a direct kind, but deliberate courses of instruction have also been devised by some schools to foster awareness of the local area. In two schools, such courses were obligatory for all pupils; in 29 they were obligatory or optional for some, while the remaining 16 had no courses of this nature, although the head of one of these said, 'problems of the community are so clearly reflected in the school that they are absorbed rather than studied'. Another said, 'they are studied incidentally in all our work'.

Special problems attracting interest included: care of the aged and handicapped; rural de-population; immigration and race relations; development of community life in new towns, etc.; unemployment and redundancy due to automation, etc.

## Community consciousness in the schools

The use of school buildings in the evenings can contribute to the life of the local community, and in only seven of the 47 schools were the buildings left unused outside school hours.

It had been expected that schools which exhibited little community awareness in some fields might compensate by showing greater awareness in others, but this proved not to be the case. In general, schools which showed the greatest activity in some fields, tended also to show high levels of activity in most others, while those organizing and planning little in the way of school functions were also relatively isolated from the community in other ways.

To close this chapter without some mention of informal contacts between parents and teachers would be unrealistic, but unless a register were kept of the number of times, if at all, the parents had been to the schools to meet the class and subject teachers and also those in more responsible positions, this would be impossible. Although these contacts do not form part of our study they are, of course, an integral and most important, although informal, part of the links and contacts between the schools and the community.

# CHAPTER EIGHT

# A Look Back and Forward

PRIMARY schools have always been comprehensive in the sense that all children in a neighbourhood, apart from those going to independent and private schools and those whose parents have exercised their right of choice, have attended the local school. Secondary comprehensive schools, however, have their origins in more recent history; they were pioneered by the Old London County Council and a few other authorities after the war. A further milestone was the introduction of the two-tier Leicestershire plan schools in 1957. The comprehensive movement seems only to have gathered momentum, however, in the early 1960s, when attention was increasingly focused on the lack of precision inherent in any testing and selection procedure (Yates and Pidgeon, 1957), on the inaccuracy of the 11-plus examinations as predictors of later attainments and on the unequal opportunities of gaining a selective school place (Douglas, 1964). In addition to these arguments, there has been growing understanding of the social structure and patterns of personal relationships within the schools and there have been strong attacks on the likely divisive effect of educating future generations in separate establishments.

Apart from a reference at the beginning to the number of authorities with approved plans for all or parts of their areas, this report, which is focused on a small group of comprehensive schools, has made no reference to the current overall position of secondary education in England and Wales. Three points are worth making from the latest available list of comprehensive schools of the Department of Education and Science (1968) (see Appendix Tables A8.1 to A8.4).

1. In January 1968 only 20 per cent of secondary pupils were attending comprehensive schools and in January 1969 the proportion was 26 per cent.

2. Although much has been written recently about middle schools (generally those bridging the years eight to nine to 12-13) and sixth-form colleges, their development is very recent. Apart from schools in

175

Leicestershire which can be variously classified, there were no middle schools in January 1968; there were 23 in January 1969, but they were concentrated in two authorities. The number of schools of this type is growing rapidly, however, and was 126 in January 1970. Sixty authorities have had plans approved which included middle schools. In January 1969 there were only six sixth-form colleges: this increased to 10 in January 1970 and plans exist for a further 34.

3. The average number of pupils in a comprehensive school at present is somewhere between 800 and 1,000, but the distribution of school size is somewhat weighted towards the smaller ones. In other words, the most usual school size is just below 800 pupils. The smallest comprehensive school is in the Isles of Scilly—this had only 79 pupils at the time of the survey and no sixth form: the largest, in Sussex, had 2,125.

This report is being written at a time of great expansion in education and the increasing interest shown by parents in the school progress of their children is noteworthy. The proportion of pupils remaining at school after the age of 16 steadily increases year by year, as do the numbers passing examinations of all types and entering courses in higher education. The long drawn-out and still continuing controversy over the organization of secondary education and the mushrooming of educational pressure groups also reflect this general interest.

It is within this setting of overall school, college and university expansion that comprehensive education is developing. As reorganization proceeds, more pupils are attending these schools, but the pattern is by no means uniform. The traditional 11-18 all-through school is still the most common type, but many local education authorities have devised and are devising schemes catering for pupils of different age-ranges.

This project, the second stage of which is reported here, has given a fuller and more detailed description of comprehensive education than was possible earlier, for the first survey was based on postal questionnaires sent to heads and their staffs (Monks, 1968). At this second stage, in 1967/68, the research team visited the schools themselves and so were able to study at first hand the broader and more complex aspects of school life. The team was struck by the variety of the schools and this heterogeneity has meant that some of the chapters have been difficult to present and summarize. Much of the rich and varied detail has had to be omitted in order to give a coherent picture.

176

The study shows that the comprehensive schools in this sample are still not receiving the expected proportion of more able pupils: only 15 of the 45 schools had 15 per cent or more of their intake of pupils in the top 20 per cent of the national population with regard to attainment and ability. The pattern of recruitment to these schools seems to have remained fairly constant over the two years 1965/66 to 1967/68. This means that any valid comparison between the progress and achievement of pupils in comprehensive and other types of secondary school is difficult to make, for the groups of pupils are not of equal ability. Only if ability is taken into account can satisfactory comparisons be made.

In spite of the relatively low proportion of able pupils, however, there is a considerable range of ability of the boys and girls in each school, from those who are academically orientated, studying for 'O' and 'A' levels, to those who need special help and encouragement with their work in order to achieve at least a minimum of literacy and numeracy. Catering for pupils of widely differing abilities and needs produces a number of apparently conflicting policies in the schools and Chapter Three has illustrated the kind of contrasts arising and the ways in which the various schools have compromised between what is ideal and what is practical.

Chapter Six has also highlighted the particular difficulties of the non-participating pupils, who take no part in the voluntary extra-curricular programme. The interests of these pupils, who tend to be of lower ability (and to a lesser extent of lower social class) are different, one assumes, from the more involved and active boys and girls. The involved pupils, in spite of heavier homework commitments and sometimes longer journeys, still manage to belong to a greater number of clubs and societies.

The stronger relationship between participation in activities and ability than between participation and social class is also seen in the results of Chapter Six. Ability shows a closer association with friendship choice than does social class. This, perhaps, is due to the basic teaching systems, streaming or banding, which are based on achievement. A complementary explanation could lie in the less accurate nature of the social class than the ability classification.

The breakdown of the school into smaller units for welfare and pastoral care was described in Chapter Two and the following chapter took up some of the points arising. Larger schools seem to have more formal arrangements for the delegation of these responsibilities, although the arrangements themselves vary considerably from school to school. The degree to which matters are dealt with in a systematic way also depends on the head and his staff—some schools tackled day-to-day problems as they arose, while in others responsibilities were more clearly assigned to particular members of staff.

Other examples of differences between schools are highlighted in the amount of educational guidance and careers advice available. Some schools were apparently able to provide an excellent counselling service with a member of staff specially appointed for this responsibility, with time and space to do this efficiently. In others, however, the advice was minimal and the teacher too involved with other commitments to spare time for this added charge.

The range of sixth-form courses and pupils is another example of the varied approaches of the schools. Pupils in some sixth-forms were all studying for 'A' levels, but in others all older pupils who wished to stay on into the sixth were transferred, and the courses provided catered for widely different levels of ability. Rigid streaming was a characteristic of some schools, but others variously banded or setted their pupils for teaching and, in at least one school, first- and second-years were taught in unstreamed classes. A further example of the variety between schools is seen in the number participating in the voluntary extra-curricular programme. For some schools and heads this was an important and vital part of the corporate life of the school, while for others it was regarded as peripheral. This was reflected in the varying numbers belonging to clubs and societies—less than two-fifths of the pupils in one school to more than three-quarters in others.

Besides the need for more information about comprehensive education and its functioning, it would also seem essential to define its particular aims—what these schools are particularly trying to do, how they are doing it and how far they are successful (Ford, 1969). This raises problems of evaluation: what should be measured and how should this be done? Although the original plans of this research included a large-scale follow-up, limitations of time and resources do not permit this.

For the final stage of the project a small group of 12 schools is being studied. This last study should be regarded as a pilot investigation which attempts to evaluate the aims of comprehensive education as these were identified by a group of theorists and teachers. This has involved the preparation of a number of special instruments designed to assess the extent to which the comprehensive schools are approaching these objectives. Later, these instruments could be used for investigations on a larger scale.

# APPENDICES

A   Tables not included in the text

B   Index scores for determining the strength of
various systems of internal school organization

C   Definitions

# APPENDIX A

# Tables not Included in the Text

A2.1 Staff-pupil ratios and percentages of part-time staff.

A2.2 The involvement of senior staff with teaching activities.

A2.3 Average number of hours per week spent on various activities as estimated by classroom teachers in different types of schools.

A2.4 Distributions of school councils and sixth-form societies among various types of schools.

A2.5 Percentages of pupils who are prefects at any one time.

A2.6 Duties of prefects.

A3.1 Social class and first-year ability bands (School 063): number of pupils.

A3.2 Social class and type of fourth-year course (School 028): number of pupils.

A4.1 Estimated percentages of 'X' and 'Z' pupils in intake.

A6.1 Social class, ability and participation: mean number of activities.

A7.1 Activities which are regularly carried out in school.

A7.2 Ex-pupil visits to schools.

A7.3 Distribution of school magazine.

A7.4 Number of schools organizing educational and vocational visits.

A7.5 Educational and vocational visits.

A8.1 Types of comprehensive schools (from DES List of Comprehensive Schools, 1968).

A8.2 Region and comprehensive schools (from DES List of Comprehensive Schools, 1968).

A8.3 Sex of pupils in comprehensive schools (from DES List of Comprehensive Schools, 1968).

A8.4 Size of comprehensive schools (from DES List of Comprehensive Schools, 1968).

## Appendix A

TABLE A2.1: *Staff-pupil ratios and percentages of part-time staff*

### Age range

| AGE RANGE | | | | STAFF-PUPIL RATIO | % OF PART-TIME STAFF |
|---|---|---|---|---|---|
| All Through (42)† .. | .. | .. | | 17·8 | 8·1 |
| Junior-High (4) | .. | .. | .. | 20·1 | 4·0 |
| Senior-High (4) | .. | .. | .. | 17·3 | 3·3 |
| *Total* (50) .. | .. | .. | .. | 18·0 | 7·4 |

### Sex

| SEX OF SCHOOL | | | | STAFF-PUPIL RATIO | % OF PART-TIME STAFF |
|---|---|---|---|---|---|
| Boys (6) | .. | .. | .. | .. | 18·1 | 5·7 |
| Girls (8) | .. | .. | .. | .. | 16·5 | 14·6 |
| Mixed (36) | | .. | .. | .. | 18·1 | 6·1 |
| *Total* (50) .. | .. | .. | .. | 18·0 | 7·4 |

### Urban/rural location

| URBAN/RURAL LOCATION | | | | STAFF-PUPIL RATIO | % OF PART-TIME STAFF |
|---|---|---|---|---|---|
| London (10) | .. | .. | .. | 16·9 | 18·2 |
| Other urban (21) .. | | .. | .. | 18·4 | 6·1 |
| Rural (19) .. | .. | .. | .. | 18·3 | 3·2 |
| *Total* (50) .. | .. | .. | .. | 18·0 | 7·4 |

### Geographical region

| GEOGRAPHICAL REGION | | | | STAFF-PUPIL RATIO | % OF PART-TIME STAFF |
|---|---|---|---|---|---|
| North (13) .. | .. | .. | .. | 18·6 | 3·3 |
| Midlands (11) | .. | .. | .. | 18·5 | 5·3 |
| Wales (9) .. | .. | .. | .. | 17·2 | 1·4 |
| South (17) .. | .. | .. | .. | 17·5 | 15·0 |
| *Total* (50) .. | .. | .. | .. | 18·0 | 7·4 |

† No of schools given in brackets.

181

TABLE A2.2: *The involvement of senior staff with teaching activities*

**Time scheduled (on timetable) for teaching**

| No. of Periods (40 Mins. Duration) | Head | Deputy Head | Senior Master/ Mistress | Head of 'School' Section or Building | Heads of Houses | Heads of Year-Groups |
|---|---|---|---|---|---|---|
| None | 13 | — | — | — | — | — |
| 1 – 5 | 13 | 4 | — | 1 | — | — |
| 6 – 10 | 15 | 9 | 5 | 4 | — | — |
| 11 – 15 | 5 | 12 | 7 | 4 | — | — |
| 16 – 20 | 1 | 3 | 9 | 2 | — | — |
| 21 – 25 | — | 7 | 5 | 1 | 6 | 2 |
| 26 – 30 | — | 10 | 10 | 2 | 5 | 4 |
| 31 – 35 | — | — | 3 | — | — | — |
| Total † | 47 | 45 | 39 | 14 | 11 | 6 |

**Time spent on marking and lesson preparation**

| Time (Hrs. per Week) | Head | Deputy Head | Senior Master/ Mistress | Head of 'School' Section or Building | Heads of Houses | Heads of Year-Groups |
|---|---|---|---|---|---|---|
| None | 10 | 3 | 1 | 2 | — | |
| 1½ hrs. or less | 11 | 3 | 3 | 4 | — | |
| 2 – 4 | 13 | 19 | 10 | 3 | 1 | Insufficient |
| 5 – 6 | 1 | 7 | 8 | 3 | 3 | information |
| 7 – 8 | 1 | 4 | 3 | 1 | 3 | |
| 9 – 10 | — | 8 | 4 | — | — | |
| Over 10 hrs. | — | 2 | 4 | 1 | 3 | |
| Total † | 36 | 46 | 33 | 14 | 10 | |

† Differences in totals are due to non-availability of information and the fact that not all positions, e.g. heads of houses, exist in all schools.

## Appendix A

TABLE A2.3: *Average number of hours per week spent on various activities estimated by classroom teachers in different types of schools*

**Size of school**

| | | ACTIVITY | | |
|---|---|---|---|---|
| SIZE OF SCHOOL | | Class Instruction | Pupil Welfare | Total Working Time |
| Up to 750 Pupils (73)†.. | .. | 18·5 | 2·3 | 41·4 |
| 751–1250 Pupils (74) .. | .. | 17·9 | 2·6 | 43·0 |
| 1251 or More Pupils (40) | .. | 17·3 | 3·2 | 45·5 |
| *All Teachers* (187) .. | .. | 18·0 | 2·6 | 42·9 |

**Urban/rural location**

| | | ACTIVITY | | |
|---|---|---|---|---|
| URBAN/RURAL LOCATION | | Class Instruction | Pupil Welfare | Total Working Time |
| London area (36) .. | .. | 16·3 | 3·5 | 42·4 |
| Other urban (80) .. | .. | 18·1 | 2·5 | 43·3 |
| Rural (71) .. .. | .. | 18·8 | 2·3 | 42·7 |
| *All Teachers* (187) .. | .. | 18·0 | 2·6 | 42·9 |

†Figures in brackets are the number of teachers in each category.

TABLE A2.4: *Distributions of school councils and sixth-form societies among various types of schools*

**Size of school**

| SIZE OF SCHOOL | NUMBER OF SCHOOLS WITH SCHOOL COUNCILS | NUMBER OF SCHOOLS WITH SIXTH-FORM SOCIETIES |
|---|---|---|
| Up to 750 Pupils (14)† | 6 | 5 |
| 751–1250 Pupils (17) .. | 8 | 7 |
| 1251 or More Pupils (11) | 7 | 7 |
| *Total* (42) .. .. | 21 | 19 |

183

*Table A2.4 continued*

**Urban/rural location**

| URBAN/RURAL LOCATION | NUMBER OF SCHOOLS WITH SCHOOL COUNCILS | NUMBER OF SCHOOLS WITH SIXTH-FORM SOCIETIES |
|---|---|---|
| London Area (9) .. | 7 | 7 |
| Other Urban (16) .. | 7 | 6 |
| Rural (17) .. .. | 7 | 6 |
| *Total* (42) .. .. | 21 | 19 |

**Geographical Region**

| GEOGRAPHICAL REGION | NUMBER OF SCHOOLS WITH SCHOOL COUNCILS | NUMBER OF SCHOOLS WITH SIXTH-FORM SOCIETIES |
|---|---|---|
| North (11) .. .. | 5 | 5 |
| Midlands (7) .. .. | 4 | — |
| Wales (8) .. .. | 1 | 3 |
| South (16) .. .. | 11 | 11 |
| *Total* (42) .. .. | 21 | 19 |

**Origin**

| ORIGIN | NUMBER OF SCHOOLS WITH WITH SCHOOL COUNCILS | NUMBER OF SCHOOLS WITH SIXTH-FORM SOCIETIES |
|---|---|---|
| Secondary Modern (8) | 7 | 8 |
| New (9) .. .. .. | 5 | 3 |
| Secondary Modern + Grammar (15) .. | 6 | 4 |
| Grammar (10) .. .. | 3 | 4 |
| *Total* (42) .. .. | 21 | 19 |

†Figures in brackets are number of schools for which this information is available or relevant.

TABLE A2.5: *Percentages of pupils who are prefects at any one time*

| % OF PUPILS | NO. OF SCHOOLS |
|---|---|
| 10 or More | 7 |
| 9 | 2 |
| 8 | 3 |
| 7 | 2 |
| 6 | 1 |
| 5 | 3 |
| 4 | 4 |
| 3 | 10 |
| 2 | 5 |
| 1 | 6 |
| 0 | 1 |
| *Total* | 44 |

TABLE A2.6: *Duties of prefects*

| DUTY | NO. OF SCHOOLS |
|---|---|
| Supervision .. .. .. .. | 41 |
| 'Welfare' Work .. .. .. .. | 5 |
| House or Year Activities .. .. | 6 |
| Hosts on Special Occasions, etc. .. | 15 |
| Supervision of House Prefects .. | 2 |
| Assembly .. .. .. .. | 4 |
| Lost Property .. .. .. .. | 2 |

TABLE A3.1: *Social class and first-year ability bands (School 063):*
*number of pupils*

I=professional, II=intermediate, III=skilled,
IV=partly-skilled, V=unskilled.

SOCIAL CLASS

|  |  |  | *I* | *II* | *III* | *IV and V* | *Not Given* | *Total* |
|---|---|---|---|---|---|---|---|---|
| Band A | .. | .. | 9 | 23 | 31 | 9 | 31 | 103 |
| Band B | .. | .. | 1 | 12 | 28 | 16 | 38 | 95 |
| *Total* .. | .. | .. | 10 | 35 | 59 | 25 | 69 | 198 |

$\chi^2=12{\cdot}39$; d.f.$=3$; p$<0{\cdot}05$

TABLE A3.2: *Social class and type of fourth-year course (School 028):*
*number of pupils*

SOCIAL CLASS

| COURSES | *I* | *II* | *III* | *IV* | *V* | *Not Given* | *Total* |
|---|---|---|---|---|---|---|---|
| Academic and Modern | 1 | 17 | 17 | 4 | — | 11 | 50 |
| Tech. and Commercial | — | 8 | 28 | 5 | 5 | 13 | 59 |
| General (early leavers) | — | 3 | 19 | 9 | 4 | 11 | 46 |
| *Total* .. .. .. | 1 | 28 | 64 | 18 | 9 | 35 | 135 |

$\chi^2=19{\cdot}22$; d.f.$=4$; p$<0{\cdot}01$

TABLE A4.1: *Estimated percentages of 'X' and 'Z' pupils in intake*

| School Code | % of 'X' Pupils Based on NF68 Scores 1967/68 | Head's Estimate of % of 'X' Pupils 1965/66 | Difference Between Estimates | % of 'Z' Pupils Based on NF68 Scores 1967/68 | Head's Estimate of % of 'Z' Pupils 1965/66 | Difference Between Estimates |
|---|---|---|---|---|---|---|
| 206 | 32 | 30 | −2 | 12 | 20 | 8 |
| 289 | 31 | 55 | 24 | 7 | 15 | 8 |
| 349 | 28 | 20 | −8 | 29 | 20 | −9 |
| 356 | 22 | 20 | −2 | 22 | 20 | −2 |
| 079 | 21 | 20 | −1 | 24 | 20 | −4 |
| 026 | 20 | 14 | −6 | 19 | 20 | 1 |
| 190 | 20 | 15 | −5 | 18 | 15 | −3 |
| 199 | 19 | 15 | −4 | 12 | 15 | 3 |
| 273 | 19 | 20 | 1 | 15 | 20 | 5 |
| 029 | 18 | 15 | −3 | 17 | 20 | 3 |
| 326 | 18 | 20 | 2 | 19 | 20 | 1 |
| 028 | 17 | 15 | −2 | 18 | 22 | 4 |
| 253 | 16 | 20 | 4 | 38 | 20 | −18 |
| 073 | 16 | 21 | 5 | 18 | 20 | 2 |
| 192 | 15 | 15 | 0 | 25 | 25 | 0 |
| 314 | 14 | 10 | −4 | 17 | 20 | 3 |
| 072 | 14 | NG | — | 30 | 33 | 3 |
| 209 | 13 | 12 | −1 | 14 | 20 | 6 |
| 299 | 13 | 5 | −8 | 24 | 20 | −4 |
| 374 | 13 | 20 | 7 | 16 | 15 | −1 |
| 083 | 13 | 20 | 7 | 31 | 10 | −21 |
| 081 | 12 | 10 | −2 | 33 | 20 | −13 |
| 063 | 11 | 20 | 9 | 31 | 20 | −11 |
| 261 | 10 | 10 | 0 | 27 | 20 | −7 |
| 280 | 10 | 5 | −5 | 8 | 20 | 12 |
| 371 | 10 | 14 | 4 | 35 | 13 | −22 |
| 014 | 10 | 10 | 0 | 23 | 25 | 2 |
| 375 | 9 | 22 | 13 | 27 | 10 | −17 |
| 270 | 9 | NG | — | 40 | 27 | −13 |
| 127 | 9 | 10 | 1 | 25 | 25 | 0 |
| 185 | 8 | 18 | 10 | 26 | 12 | −14 |
| 107 | 7 | 17 | 10 | 27 | 22 | −5 |
| 125 | 6 | 20 | 14 | 32 | 20 | −12 |
| 136 | 6 | 8 | 2 | 32 | 33 | 1 |
| 171 | 6 | NG | — | 41 | NG | — |
| 317 | 5 | 7 | 2 | 42 | 18 | −24 |
| 264 | 4 | 24 | 20 | 29 | 17 | −12 |
| 158 | 4 | 9 | 5 | 45 | 28 | −17 |
| 050 | 4 | 3 | −1 | 49 | 37 | −12 |
| 049 | 4 | 0 | −4 | 44 | 34 | −10 |
| 220 | 3 | 5 | 2 | 22 | 10 | −12 |
| 093 | 2 | 5 | 3 | 35 | 20 | −15 |
| 163 | 1 | 1 | 0 | 58 | 20 | −38 |
| 166 | 1 | 8 | 7 | 47 | 40 | −7 |
| 338 | 1 | 20 | 19 | 60 | 30 | −30 |

NG = Not given.

TABLE A6.1: *Social class, ability and participation: mean number of activities*

| ESTIMATED ABILITY | | | SOCIAL CLASS | | | | |
|---|---|---|---|---|---|---|---|
| | | | *I and II* | *III* | *IV* | *V* | *All* |
| School 125 | 1 | .. | 1·27 | 0·79 | 0·86 | 0·67† | 0·98 |
| | 2 | .. | 0·79 | 0·78 | 0·52 | 0·00† | 0·75 |
| | 3 | .. | 0·55 | 0·54 | 0·35 | 0·36 | 0·51 |
| | 4 | .. | 0·44 | 0·40 | 0·42 | 0·28 | 0·40 |
| | 5 | .. | 0·33† | 0·28 | 0·40 | 0·00† | 0·29 |
| | *All* | .. | 0·81 | 0·58 | 0·46 | 0·30 | 0·61 |
| School 185 | 1 | .. | 1·36 | 1·85 | 2·08 | 1·81 | 1·78 |
| | 2 | .. | 0·86 | 0·84 | 0·94 | 0·97 | 0·88 |
| | 3 | .. | 0·71† | 0·66 | 0·56 | 0·87 | 0·70 |
| | 4 | .. | 0·17† | 0·26 | 0·43 | 0·16 | 0·24 |
| | 5 | .. | 0·00† | 0·00 | 0·17† | 0·18 | 0·08 |
| | *All* | .. | 1·02 | 0·94 | 0·89 | 0·81 | 0·91 |
| School 209 | 1 | .. | 2·58 | 2·80 | 3·86† | 3·25† | 2·79 |
| | 2 | .. | 2·46 | 2·33 | 2·59 | 2·75† | 2·44 |
| | 3 | .. | 2·00 | 2·28 | 2·60 | 2·50† | 2·26 |
| | 4 | .. | 1·60 | 2·00 | 2·56 | 3·00† | 2·20 |
| | 5 | .. | 1·77 | 2·90 | 1·75 | 2·00† | 2·05 |
| | *All* | .. | 2·32 | 2·44 | 2·53 | 2·81 | 2·42 |
| School 314 | 1 | .. | 2·18 | 1·90 | 2·33 | 2·37 | 2·03 |
| | 2 | .. | 1·62 | 1·43 | 1·19 | 1·55† | 1·41 |
| | 3 | .. | 1·14 | 1·38 | 1·39 | 2·06 | 1·42 |
| | 4 | .. | 0·83† | 1·23 | 1·26 | 1·44 | 1·24 |
| | 5 | .. | 0·50† | 0·58 | 0·56 | 0·27 | 0·52 |
| | *All* | .. | 1·61 | 1·39 | 1·36 | 1·35 | 1·40 |
| School 317 | 1 | .. | 1·54 | 1·51 | 1·92 | 0·78† | 1·50 |
| | 2 | .. | 1·53 | 1·35 | 1·27 | 1·22 | 1·35 |
| | 3 | .. | 1·91 | 0·99 | 0·87 | 1·40 | 1·11 |
| | 4 | .. | 1·00† | 0·89 | 1·14 | 0·32 | 0·86 |
| | 5 | .. | 0·00† | 0·25 | 1·00† | 0·71† | 0·34 |
| | *All* | .. | 1·59 | 1·13 | 1·24 | 0·92 | 1·16 |

†Categories with fewer than 10 pupils.

TABLE A7.1: *Activities which are regularly carried out in school*

NUMBER OF SCHOOLS WITH THIS ACTIVITY

| ACTIVITY | Geographical Area | | | | Origin | | | Total |
|---|---|---|---|---|---|---|---|---|
| | North | Midland | South | Wales | New | With Grammar | Without Grammar | |
| Prize-Giving Day | 12 | 11 | 9 | 6 | 10 | 17 | 11 | 38 |
| Athletic Events | 14 | 13 | 11 | 7 | 11 | 23 | 11 | 45 |
| Social Evening and/or Parties | 9 | 11 | 10 | 6 | *10 | 20 | 6 | 36 |
| Exhibition of Pupils' Work | *9 | 12 | 10 | 2 | 8 | 16 | 9 | 33 |
| Performance (Musical or Theatrical) by Pupils | 13 | 14 | 11 | 7 | ***11 | 24 | 10 | 45 |
| Christmas Festivities | 11 | 13 | 9 | 6 | 9 | 19 | 11 | 39 |
| Easter Festivities | **0 | 6 | 2 | 0 | 1 | 4 | 3 | 8 |
| Open Days | ***10 | 12 | 9 | 0 | 8 | 14 | 9 | 31 |
| Summer or Spring Fêtes | *5 | 9 | 10 | 2 | 5 | 14 | 7 | 26 |
| Careers Convention | 8 | 9 | 8 | 6 | 8 | 18 | 5 | 31 |
| Commemoration Day | 1 | 3 | 3 | 2 | 0 | 7 | 2 | 9 |
| 'School at Work' | 1 | 0 | 1 | 0 | 0 | 2 | 0 | 2 |
| Other | 5 | 5 | 5 | 3 | 5 | 10 | 3 | 18 |
| *Total Number of Schools* | 14 | 14 | 12 | 7 | 11 | 24 | 12 | 47 |
| Mean No. of These Activities | *7·0 | 8·4 | 8·2 | 6·7 | 7·9 | 7·8 | 7·3 | 7·7 |
| SD | 2·0 | 1·4 | 1·5 | 0·8 | 1·6 | 1·4 | 2·2 | 1·5 |

*, **, *** These distributions differ from those to be expected, with probabilities p<0·05; 0·01 and 0·001 respectively.

189

TABLE A7.2: *Ex-pupil visits to schools*

| NUMBER OF VISITS PER 1000 PUPILS ON ROLL | NUMBER OF SCHOOLS |
|---|---|
| 0–25 | 9 |
| 26–50 | 10 |
| 51–75 | 8 |
| 76–100 | 5 |
| 101–125 | 5 |
| 176–200 | 1 |
| 201–250 | 1 |
| No Reply | 8 |
| *Total* | 47 |

TABLE A7.3: *Distribution of school magazine*

| NUMBER OF COPIES PER 100 PUPILS ON ROLL | NUMBER OF SCHOOLS |
|---|---|
| 0–25 | 2 |
| 26–50 | 4 |
| 51–75 | 7 |
| 76–100 | 8 |
| 101–125 | 5 |
| 126–150 | — |
| 151–175 | 2 |
| 625–650 | 1 |
| No Figures Available | 7 |
| No Magazine | 11 |
| *Total* | 47 |

TABLE A7.4: *Number of schools organizing educational and vocational visits*

| | EDUCATIONAL | VOCATIONAL |
|---|---|---|
| Regularly, as school policy | 33 | 36 |
| Occasionally .. | 8 | 3 |
| Less than the head would like | 3 | 5 |
| Organized by individual teachers .. | 3 | 3 |

TABLE A7.5: *Educational and vocational visits*

ESTIMATED NO. OF SCHOOL EDUCATIONAL VISITS ORGANIZED IN 1966/67

| Visits | | | | 1–10 | 11–20 | 21–30 | 41–50 | 51–60 | 91–100 | No reply | Total |
|---|---|---|---|---|---|---|---|---|---|---|---|
| Schools | | | | 16 | 18 | 1 | 3 | 2 | 1 | 6 | 47 |

ESTIMATED PERCENTAGE OF SCHOOL ROLL SENT ON VISITS IN 1966/67

| | | 1–10 | 11–20 | 21–30 | 31–40 | 41–50 | 61–70 | 71–80 | 81–90 | 91–100 | No reply | Total |
|---|---|---|---|---|---|---|---|---|---|---|---|---|
| Educational visits | | 2 | 7 | 10 | 6 | 4 | 3 | 2 | 1 | 6 | 6 | 47 |
| Vocational visits | | 13 | 12 | 7 | 5 | 3 | | 2 | | 2 | 3 | 47 |

AVERAGE PERCENTAGE OF SCHOOL ROLL SENT ON EDUCATIONAL VISITS

| *Geographical Area* | | | | *North* | *Midlands* | *South* | *Wales* | *All* |
|---|---|---|---|---|---|---|---|---|
| Mean | .. | .. | .. | 28·0 | 51·5 | 67·2 | 27·8 | 43·5 |
| SD | .. | .. | .. | 17·4 | 18·6 | 33·5 | 9·5 | 29·9 |
| No. of Schools | .. | .. | .. | 13 | 11 | 11 | 6 | 41 |

| *Origin of School* | | | | *New* | *Grammar* | *Non-Grammar* | *All* |
|---|---|---|---|---|---|---|---|
| Mean | .. | .. | .. | 45·1 | 28·0 | 55·1 | 43·5 |
| SD | .. | .. | .. | 29·6 | 39·0 | 25·2 | 29·9 |
| No. of Schools | .. | .. | .. | 10 | 21 | 10 | 41 |

| *Sex of Pupils* | | | | *Boys* | *Girls* | *Mixed* | *All* |
|---|---|---|---|---|---|---|---|
| Mean | .. | .. | .. | 28·7 | 66·9 | 39·9 | 43·5 |
| SD | .. | .. | .. | 15·6 | 33·3 | 27·4 | 29·9 |
| No. of Schools | .. | .. | .. | 6 | 8 | 27 | 41 |

TABLE A8.1: *Types of comprehensive schools (from DES List of Comprehensive Schools, 1968)*

| TYPE OF SCHOOL | NO. OF SCHOOLS | % OF TOTAL | NO. OF PUPILS | % OF TOTAL |
|---|---|---|---|---|
| All-Through (inc. 11-16) .. .. | 515 | 69 | 484,989 | 80 |
| JHS .. .. .. .. | 153 | 20 | 74,624 | 12 |
| SHS .. .. .. .. | 77 | 10 | 43,837 | 7 |
| Sixth-Form Colleges .. .. | 3 | 1 | 2,129 | 1 |
| Middle Schools .. .. .. | 0 | 0 | 0 | 0 |
| *Total* .. .. .. .. | 748 | 100 | 605,579 | 100 |
| No. of Pupils in Secondary Schools† .. .. | | | 2,930,000 | |
| % of Secondary Pupils in Comprehensive Schools .. .. | | | 20 | |

† Projection, based on DES Statistics of Education, 1967 and a 3·4 per cent annual growth.

TABLE A8.2: *Region and comprehensive schools (from DES List of Comprehensive Schools, 1968)*

| GEOGRAPHICAL REGION | ALL-THROUGH | JUNIOR HIGH | SENIOR HIGH | SIXTH-FORM COLLEGES | TOTAL |
|---|---|---|---|---|---|
| *North* (Lancs, Yorks and points north to Scotland) .. | 160 | 40 | 23 | 1 | 224 |
| *Midlands* (Hereford to Ipswich up to 'North') .. .. | 60 | 41 | 17 | 0 | 118 |
| *Wales* .. .. .. | 66 | 35 | 17 | 0 | 118 |
| *South* (Hereford to Ipswich and points south) .. .. | 229 | 37 | 20 | 2 | 288 |
| *Total* .. .. .. | 515 | 153 | 77 | 3 | 748 |

TABLE A8.3: *Sex of pupils in comprehensive schools (from DES List of Comprehensive Schools, 1968)*

| SEX OF SCHOOLS | NO. OF SCHOOLS | % OF TOTAL |
|---|---|---|
| Boys | 83 | 12 |
| Girls | 81 | 12 |
| Mixed | 584 | 76 |
| *Total* | 748 | 100 |

TABLE A8.4: *Size of comprehensive schools (from DES List of Comprehensive Schools, 1968)*

| SIZE OF SCHOOLS | | ALL-THROUGH | JUNIOR HIGH | SENIOR HIGH | SIXTH-FORM COLLEGES | TOTAL |
|---|---|---|---|---|---|---|
| up to 400 pupils | .. | 31 | 55 | 5 | — | 91 |
| 401–600 | .. .. | 72 | 53 | 42 | 2 | 169 |
| 601–800 | .. .. | 108 | 34 | 17 | — | 159 |
| 801–1000 | .. .. | 95 | 8 | 11 | 1 | 115 |
| 1001–1200 | .. .. | 93 | 3 | 2 | — | 98 |
| 1201–1400 | .. .. | 45 | — | — | — | 45 |
| 1401–1600 | .. .. | 30 | — | — | — | 30 |
| 1601–1800 | .. .. | 22 | — | — | — | 22 |
| 1801–2000 | .. .. | 16 | — | — | — | 16 |
| 2001–2200 | .. .. | 3 | — | — | — | 3 |
| *Total* | .. .. | 515 | 153 | 77 | 3 | 748 |
| Mean .. | .. .. | 943 | 475 | 600 | — | |
| SD .. | .. .. | 396 | 214 | 190 | — | |

# Index Scores for Determining the Strength of Various Systems of Internal School Organization

THE INDEX score was devised to estimate the strength of various organizational systems within the schools. The organizational *system* is identified principally by the title of the staff involved with the general welfare of pupils (e.g. heads of houses, senior masters, etc.). The *strength* of the system is measured first by the extent to which these senior teachers are involved with the general welfare of pupils, and second by the practical support these posts receive in time, money, and building provision.

### Pupil welfare activities

Ten specific activities concerned with the general welfare of pupils and common to most schools in the survey were considered. Senior teachers[1] were asked which members of staff were involved with each activity.

Each level of staff in each school received on the basis of the senior teachers' replies a score running from 0 to 3, i.e. not involved to heavily involved. These scores were later scaled so that each activity constituted five per cent of the total maximum score and the 10 activities together constituted 50 per cent of the total index score. (If a representative of a level of staff was not interviewed or could not give a reliable estimate of the numbers involved, the score was determined by the number of senior teachers interviewed who indicated that this particular level of staff was involved. If they both indicated that the same level of staff was involved with a particular activity, that level of staff scored three. If both indicated different levels of staff, a score of one was given to each of the two levels of staff mentioned.)

For the traditional system's scores, the scores for head, deputy

---

[1] Full-time teaching staff with a comparatively reduced teaching load, in positions of administrative authority. These would normally include senior masters or mistresses, heads of lower, middle or upper school, housemasters, etc. It was left to the head to decide which two of his staff should be interviewed.

head, senior masters and/or mistresses, and heads of subject department or form teachers were added together and divided by three (the head, deputy head, and senior master or mistress).

## Allowances

The award of extra allowances was seen as a useful indicator of the official status of an organizational system. One point was given, up to a maximum of 10 points, for each per cent of the school's total allowances awarded solely for organizational duties to a particular level of staff. Thus if a school received a total of 100 allowance points (see Chapter Two) of which eight were devoted to house teachers specifically for these responsibilities, the house system scored eight points.

For the traditional system, the number of points awarded to the senior master and/or mistress were taken, but not those awarded to the head or deputy head, since they were not included in the calculations of allowance points.

Scores for allowances were scaled so that they constituted approximately 17 per cent of the total index scores.

## Time

One point was given for every half-period less than the school average for heads of subject departments that the levels of staff responsible for an organizational system taught. Thus, if heads of subject departments in a school averaged 25 periods a week while heads of houses averaged 22 periods, the house system was awarded six points.

For the traditional system, the time that the senior master or mistress taught was taken, and the teaching time of the head and deputy head ignored.

Scores for time were scaled to equal about 17 per cent of the total index score.

## Buildings

A school with purpose-built blocks, with separate dining, teaching and staff facilities, whatever organizational system the blocks were built for, scored 10. If a school had buildings on two sites more than half a mile apart, this was seen as favouring a lower/upper school system of organization, and a score of seven points was awarded. Similarly, if the school had two separate sites which were less than half a mile apart, a 'school' system was awarded five points. If, however, a school had separate, distinct blocks, without common facilities, but on one site, this was still seen as favouring a 'school', year or building system, and whichever of these was reflected in the allowance structure was awarded an additional three points on account of the building provision. When the majority of the school was accommodated in a single block, this was seen as favouring the more centralized 'traditional' system, and five points were allocated.

The scaled scores derived from the building provision constituted approximately 17 per cent of the total index score.

### 'Strong' and 'weak' systems

The index score is to a certain extent influenced by the size of the school. It is also probable that the strength of the traditional system is not accurately reflected in a comparable way, since the scores derived from allowances and buildings make it more difficult for a high score for the traditional system to be achieved. Therefore comparison between scores of various systems *within* each school is likely to be more valid than comparisons *between* schools.

Schools fall into three clear groups regarding house systems— 'strong', 'weak' and 'none'. The strong group includes those with scores of 50 points or more for this system. Seven schools had scores ranging from 12 to 35—weak house systems. The remaining 32 schools, however, had house system scores of 10 or less. (These schools may, or course, have strong house systems for purposes other than those defined in this report, e.g. games, assembly.)

For school systems 13 schools had scores of 50 or above—these had strong 'school' systems. A further three scored between 20-30; these are classified as having weak 'school' systems.

For year systems the divisions were less clear-cut, but in no instance was the year system the dominant form of organization. It would appear safe to consider scores of 50 or more as indicating a strong organizational system.

### Conclusions

Within the limitations of this study, the index seems to provide an objective and adequate measure of relative strengths of various systems of school organization. It is also able to cope with the complexity of several systems of organization operating simultaneously within the same school.

*Appendix B*

## Scale for determining strengths of systems

*Activities*

1. *Truancy*
   no. of interviewees,† max. 3

2. *Contact with parents (per year)*
   |  |  |
   |---|---|
   | 0 – 9 | scores 0 |
   | 10 – 79 | 1 |
   | 80 – 199 | 2 |
   | 200 or more | 3 |

3. *Contact with pupils (per week)*
   |  |  |
   |---|---|
   | 0 – 9 | scores 0 |
   | 10 – 14 | 1 |
   | 15 – 24 | 2 |
   | 25 or more | 3 |

4. *Reports to employment*
   (or no. of interviews)
   |  |  |
   |---|---|
   | 1 – 30 | scores 1 |
   | 31 – 90 | 2 |
   | 91 or more | 3 |

5. *Supervision of end of term reports*
   |  |  |
   |---|---|
   | 1 – 30 | scores 1 |
   | 31 – 120 | 2 |
   | 121 or more | 3 |

6. *Courses*
   (or no. of interviews)
   |  |  |
   |---|---|
   | 1 – 30 | scores 1 |
   | 31 – 120 | 2 |
   | 121 or more | 3 |

7. *Careers*
   (or no. of interviews)
   |  |  |
   |---|---|
   | 1 – 10 | scores 1 |
   | 11 – 60 | 2 |
   | 61 or more | 3 |

8. *New intake*
   |  |  |
   |---|---|
   | 1 – 30 | scores 1 |
   | 31 –120 | 2 |
   | 121 or more | 3 |

9. *Sick pupils (per week)*
   |  |  |
   |---|---|
   | 1 – 4 | scores 1 |
   | 5 – 24 | 2 |
   | 25 or more | 3 |

10. *Stealing*
    no. of interviewees,† max. 3

† No. of interviewees=no. of senior teachers indicating that the relevant level of staff was involved.

*Allowances*
One point for every percentage of allowance for 'organization' post (max. 10).

*Time*
One point for every half-period less than heads of subject department (max. 10).

| *Building* | *Score* |
| --- | --- |
| Purpose-built blocks, with separate dining, teaching and staff facilities .. .. .. .. .. .. .. | 10 |
| Blocks separated by more than half a mile.. .. .. | 7 |
| Blocks on different sites, separated up to half a mile apart .. | 5 |
| Separate, distinct blocks, on one site, without common facilities .. .. .. .. .. .. .. .. | 3 |

# APPENDIX C

# Definitions

*Ability*

Schools were asked to classify their pupils into one of five categories each to include approximately 20 per cent of the total. These ability categories are designated from I to V in descending order of ability.

*Social Class*

Pupils were allocated to the five classes of the Registrar-General's classification by parental occupation:

> I – Professional
> II – Intermediate
> III – Skilled
> IV – Partly-skilled
> V – Unskilled.

*Behaviour*

I – pupils who have never or seldom had 'brushes' with the administration of the school;

II – pupils who have shown some (average) behavioural difficulties of an ordinary kind;

III – pupils who have shown behavioural difficulties that the school has not been able to deal with and/or has needed specialist outside help;

IV – pupils who have appeared in Court.

*Ethnic Origin*

> I – British White
> II – European
> III – Coloured
> IV – Other

199

# LIST OF REFERENCES

ASSOCIATION OF EDUCATION COMMITTEES. (1965). School Library Allowances and Allowances for School Textbooks, Stationery and Materials. (Extract from Executive Minutes, Ref. No. 272, 25th March 1965.)

BARKER LUNN, J. C. (1970). *Streaming in the Primary School.* Slough: NFER.

BLYTH, W. A. L. (1960). 'The sociometric study of children's groups in English schools', *Brit. J. Educ. Studs.*, **8**, 1, 127-47.

CRISWELL, J. H. (1943). 'Sociometric methods of measuring group preferences', *Sociometry*, **6**, 4, 398-408.

DEPARTMENT OF EDUCATION AND SCIENCE. (1965). *The Organization of Secondary Education.* Circular 10/65. London: HM Stationery Office.

DEPARTMENT OF EDUCATION AND SCIENCE. (1967). *Scales of Salaries for Teachers in Primary and Secondary Schools in England and Wales.* London: HM Stationery Office.

DEPARTMENT OF EDUCATION AND SCIENCE. (1967). *Comprehensive Schools from Existing Buildings* (Building Bulletin 40). London: HM Stationery Office.

DEPARTMENT OF EDUCATION AND SCIENCE: CENTRAL ADVISORY COUNCIL FOR EDUCATION (ENGLAND). (1967). *Children and their Primary Schools* (Plowden Report). London: HM Stationery Office.

DEPARTMENT OF EDUCATION AND SCIENCE. (1967). *Statistics of Education.* London: HM Stationery Office.

DEPARTMENT OF EDUCATION AND SCIENCE. (1968). *Statistics of Education.* Special Series, Survey of the Curriculum and Deployment of Teachers (Secondary Schools, 1965-66, Part 1). London: HM Stationery Office.

DEPARTMENT OF EDUCATION AND SCIENCE. (1968). List of Comprehensive Schools in England and Wales. Duplicated sheets.

DOUGLAS, J. W. B. (1964). *The Home and the School.* London: MacGibbon & Kee.

FORD, J. (1969). *Social Class and the Comprehensive School.* London: Routledge & Kegan Paul.

HARGREAVES, D. H. (1967). *Social Relations in a Secondary School.* London: Routledge & Kegan Paul.

HIMMELWEIT, H. T. (1966). 'Social background, intelligence and school structure'. Chapter in: MEADE, J. E. and PARKES, A. S. eds. *Genetic and Environmental Factors in Human Ability.* Edinburgh: Oliver & Boyd.

KAWWA, T. (1963). 'Ethnic prejudice and choice of friends amongst English and non-English adolescents'. Unpublished MA thesis, University of London.

KAWWA, T. (1965). 'A study of the interaction between native and immigrant children in an English school, with special reference to ethnic prejudice'. Unpublished PhD thesis, University of London.

MINISTRY OF EDUCATION: CENTRAL ADVISORY COUNCIL FOR EDUCATION (ENGLAND). (1963). *Half Our Future* (Newsom Report). London: HM Stationery Office.

## List of References

MONKS, T. G. (1968). *Comprehensive Education in England and Wales*. Slough: NFER.

MORENO, J. L., *et al.* (1960). *The Sociometry Reader*. Chicago, Illinois: Free Press.

NATIONAL FOUNDATION FOR EDUCATIONAL RESEARCH. (1969). *Trends in Allocation Procedures*. Slough: NFER.

SCHOOLS COUNCIL. (1969). *The 1966 CSE Monitoring Experiment* (Working Paper No. 21). London: HM Stationery Office.

SCHOOL LIBRARY ASSOCIATION. (1961). *School Libraries Today*. London: SLA.

YOUNG, M. and MCGEENEY, P. (1968). *Learning Begins at Home*. London: Routledge & Kegan Paul.

YATES, A. and PIDGEON, D. A. (1957). *Admission to Grammar Schools*. London: Newnes (refer NFER).

YATES, A. (1966). *Grouping in Education*. Stockholm: Almqvist and Wiksell; New York: Wiley (for Unesco Institute for Education, Hamburg).

A selected annotated bibliography on Comprehensive Education is forthcoming (available from NFER, Slough),

# Index of Proper Names

Association of Education Committees 96, 200

Barker Lunn, J. C. 69, 200

Bates, A. W. 5, 25

Blyth, W. A. L. 118, 200

Careers Advisory Service 84

Central Advisory Council for Education 128, 200

Connaughton, I. M. 101

Criswell, J. H. 119, 200

Department of Education and Science 17, 40, 52, 175, 200

Department of Education and Science (Cardiff) 7

Douglas, J. W. B. 69, 175, 200

Ford, J. 118, 178, 200

Evison, P. 5, 100

Hargreaves, D. H. 118, 200

Heim, A. W. 100

Himmelweit, H. T. 69, 200

HM Inspectorate for Wales 7, 101

James, I. L. 7

Kawwa, T. 5, 118, 169, 200

Liverpool, University of, Sociology Department 18

London County Council 175

Manchester, University of, Department of Education 18

Monks, T. G. 5, 17, 20, 26, 70, 85, 94, 129, 169, 176, 201

Moon, J. 5, 8

Moreno, J. L. 118, 201

McGeeney, P. 169, 201

National Federation of Parent-Teacher Associations 170

National Foundation for Educational Research 24, 62, 98, 201

Newsom, Sir John 128

Pidgeon, D. A. 7, 10, 175

Reid, M. I. 5, 128

Robertson, T. S. 5, 60, 118, 169

Ross, J. M. 5, 10

Rossetti, H. F. 18

School Library Association 96, 201

Schools Council 101, 201

Secretary of State for Education & Science 17, 18

Skurnik, L. S. 101

Vernon, P. E. 100, 101

Watts, A. F. 100

Wiseman, S. 7, 10

Yates, A. 175, 201

Young, P. 169, 201

Youth Employment Bureau 74

Youth Employment Service 84

202

# General Index

Ability Grouping  61, 98
    1st year  63-69
    4th year  74-78
Ability Group
    definitions  199
    popularity  120, 126, 127
    in-group preference  121-127
    extra-curricular activities  148-155
Able Pupils
    see 'X' pupils
    ability group
Activities, voluntary extra-curricular
    see 'extra-curricular activities'
Activities, School
    see school functions
Administration  17, 25-59
    classroom teacher  48-52
    duties of senior staff  40-47
    house system  36
    internal organization  35-36
    role of pupils  53
    salary allowances  26, 31-35
    school & year systems  37
    source & methods of research
      23, 25
    staffing  25-26
    summary  54
    traditional system  36
Agricultural Science  79
AH4 Group Test of Intelligence  100
Aims & Objectives  18-19
'A' Level  86-90
Allocation on Entry  62-63
Allowances, Staff Salaries  26-35, 55,
  195
All-through Schools (11-18 Schools)
  108, 181, 192, 193, 172
Aptitude, Test of Scholastic
    see CP66
Arithmetic Test
    see NF68, Vernon Graded
      Arithmetic/Mathematics Test
Art  72, 79, 80, 89, 92, 93
    gallery visits  172

Arts
    sixth form  90
Athletic Events  169
Attainment Survey  100-117
    source & methods  23

Bands, Ability  66-70, 74, 80, 98
Behavioural Groups
    definitions  199
    popularity  120
    in-group preference  122, 124
Biology  80, 82, 89, 92, 93
Bipartite System  32, 98
Boarding Pupils  38
Botany  89
Boys' Schools  181
Buildings, School
    converting for comprehensive
      purposes  40
    effect on organization  38, 56
    maintenance  25
    index  195
Burnham Reports  26, 55
    see allowances, staff salary

Careers
    advice  56, 74, 83-85, 98
    conventions  169
    course  80
Chemistry  78, 80, 89, 91, 92
Circular, 10/65  17, 20, 25, 200
Clerical Duties  48
College Entrance  84
Coloured Pupils  119
Commercial
    courses  76, 80, 88, 92
    visits  172
Community Contacts  169-174
    non-teaching staff  173
    parent-teacher associations  170
    relationships with former pupils
      170
    relationships with other schools
      and educational organizations
      171

203

school courses on community
relationships 173
school functions and activities
169
school magazines 171
source and methods 23
visits, to factories, farms and
commercial firms 172
voluntary social work 173
Comprehensive Education
evaluation, aims and objectives
18-19
Consultation 73, 79, 81
Contacts with Community
*see* community contacts
Counsellors 70
Courses, 4th year 74, 76, 81
CP66, Test of General Scholastic Aptitude, description of 101
first-year sixth results 104
Craft 72
CSE 41, 73, 74, 79, 90, 91, 101, 171
Current Affairs 78
Curriculum
1st–3rd years 72
4th–5th years 78
6th form 85 *et seq.*
co-ordination 171
method, source of information 23
planning 45
summary 97

Day release
pupils on 172
Delegation of responsibility 57
Deputy Head
*see* senior staff
Design 76
Discussion Groups 171
Domestic Science
*see* housecraft
Drama 73, 80

Economics 89, 91, 92
Educational Visits 172
Engineering 76
drawing 91, 92
English 72, 78-82, 89-93
teachers 51
English Reading Test
*see* NF68
Watts-Vernon
Ethnic Origin
definition 199
popularity of different groups 120

Examinations
*see* public examination, GCE,
CSE, A-level, O-level
setting 48
Exhibitions, of work 169
visits to 172
Extra-Curricular Activities 17, 49
contribution of teaching staff
163
functions of 130
non-participants 141
participation and year group 142
organization 134, 165
participation of ability groups
148
participation of boys and girls
147
participation and environmental
factors 159
participation of social classes
155
pupil participation 140, 167
source & methods 23, 129
summary 165

Factory Visits 172
Family Care 80
Farm Visits 172
Fêtes 169, 170
Follow-up
*see* Plowden, of pupils in com-
prehensive schools 73, 98
Former Pupils
visits to school 170, 190
Form Periods 79
Form Teachers
and settling down 70
French 64, 72, 79-82, 89-93
Friendships 118-127
Functions & Activities 169, 189

Games 72, 78, 79
GCE 73, 74
*see* A-level, O-level
General Course 76, 80
General Studies 90
General Sixth 90
Geographical Differences
ability of pupils 110
age range 192
educational visits 172
pupils' role in school administration 54
school councils 184
school functions 169, 189

sixth-form societies   184
staff-pupil ratios   181
time spent in teaching   52
Geography   72, 78-80, 89-93
teachers   51
German   72, 80-82, 89-92
Girls' Schools   143, 181, 193
Grammar Schools, former   52, 78, 85-86, 90, 96, 106-107, 170, 171, 184, 189
Graduates
hours worked   51
Graded Posts
see Burnham Reports
Greek Civilization   92
Guidance
see Careers Advice
Consultation
Counsellors
Pupil welfare
summary   97
Handicraft   72
Head boy/girl   53, 58
Head Teacher
and pupil welfare   36
duties   41
see also Senior Staff
Heads of Departments
salary allowances   28
Head of Lower School   31, 34, 39, 70, 71, 182
Head of Middle School   34, 35, 39, 182
Head of Upper School
allowances   31
duties   182
Heads of Years
see Year teachers
History   72, 78, 80, 82, 89-92
teachers   51
Home economics   92
see also Housecraft
Housecraft (Domestic Science)   73, 79-80, 89
see also home economics
House masters
and careers advice   84
staff allowances   31
duties   182
House System   37, 56, 70
staff allowances   31
and extra-curricular activities   136
ILEA schools   20, 83, 96, 106-110, 172, 181, 183, 184

Index of Preference   119
Intelligence
see AH4 Group Test of Intelligence
NF68
'X' ability pupils
'Z' ability pupils
International affairs   80
Interviews
see Methods of Research, of parents by teachers   43
Journeys   171
Junior High Schools   26, 29, 76, 106-109, 143, 172, 181, 192
Junior school profile   71
Large Schools   32, 34, 36, 37, 46, 49, 58, 66, 69, 79, 80, 88, 94, 98, 172, 183, 184
Latin   35, 72, 78, 89
Leavers   74, 84
Leisure studies   80
Lesson preparation   48-53
Libraries
school   95-97, 99
Local Education Authorities
and Circular 10/65, 17
and Burnham Reports   27, 55
Lower School
see school systems
head of lower school
Magazines, school   190
Marking
by classroom teachers   48
Mathematics   35, 72, 78, 81, 82, 89, 91, 92, 93
and staff allowances   31
teachers   51
test, see NF68 and Vernon Graded Arithmetic
Matron, school   44, 57
Metalwork   73, 80, 81, 82, 89, 91, 92
Methods of research   23, 25, 36, 48, 60, 100, 118, 129
Middle schools   175, 193
Minority-time subjects   90, 91
Mixed ability groups   74
see also unstreaming
Mixed schools   171, 181, 193
Mixing of abilities   81
Modern Languages   72
teachers   51
see also French, German, Spanish, Russian
Modern Society   80

205

Motor mechanics 80, 82
Museums, visits 172
Music 72, 79, 80, 82, 89
    competitions between schools 171
Musical performances 169
Needlework 79, 80, 82
NF68 Test 100-101, 102, 103, 112
Non-academic subjects 55
    *see also* practical subjects
Non-graduates
    hours worked 51
Nurses
    *see* Matrons
NS71 Welsh reading test 101
O-level 42, 74, 79, 90, 91, 101
Open days 169
Option-blocks 62, 74-81, 91-92
Organization, internal 35-59
Parental occupation
    *see* social class
Parents' meetings 57, 170
Parent-Teacher Associations 170
Party evenings 169
Physical education 72, 78, 79, 82
Physics 78-82, 89, 91, 92
Plowden follow-up study 100, 102
Plowden Report 102, 169
Points score
    *see* allowances
Policy 48
    -making, pupil involvement 59
    towards extra-curricular activity
    130
Popularity
    of different pupils 119
Pottery 73, 80
Practical subjects 73, 78, 79
    and special allowances 31
    teachers 51
Practitioners (educational) 18
Prefects 53, 58, 93, 185
Preference
    *see* Index of Preference
    in-group and out-group 121
Primary schools 63
Privileges
    sixth-form 93
Public affairs 92
    *see also* current affairs
                international affairs
Public examinations 41
    *see* CSE, GCE, O-level, A-level
Public relations 45, 49
    response to invitations 170

Pupil responsibilities 53
Pupil welfare 44, 48, 70
    *see also* careers guidance
                consultation
    additional staff allowances 31
    arrangements 42
    index 194
    organization 36 *et seq.*
    source and methods 23
    time spent 51, 58
Purpose-built schools 37, 40
Quota system 26
Reading Test
    *see* NF68, Watts Vernon English
        Reading Test, Welsh 7
Reception
    *see* settling down
Records of pupils 48
Regional differences
    *see* geographical differences
Religious education 72, 78, 79, 80,
    82, 89
Remedial classes
    special staff allowances 31
Reports
    *see* School Profile
    writing school reports 43, 57
Responsibilities
    sixth form pupils' 93
    allowances to staff 31
    of staff 35
Rural schools 32, 35, 38, 58, 63, 83,
    85, 110, 155, 172, 181, 183, 184
Russian 72, 89
Schemes
    comprehensive education 17
Schools council 53, 59, 183
School systems 70
    traditional 36
    house 37
    school and year 37
Science
    1st-3rd years 72
    general 78
    rural 80, 82
    4th year 80, 82
    sixth 90
    staff allowances 31
    agricultural 79
Scripture
    *see* Religious education
Secondary modern, former 53, 85,
    86, 96, 107, 171, 184, 189

Senior high school 29, 76, 108, 143, 172, 181, 192
Senior Staff
    duties 40-47, 182
    time spent with abler pupils 95
    salary allowances 28
    and pupil welfare 36
    index 194
Sets, subject 64, 78, 80
Settling down 39, 44
Sick pupils 44
Single-sex schools 85, 171
    *see also* boys' schools, girls' schools
Sixth form 17, 29, 34, 53, 85-99, 142, 171, 175, 183, 192
Size of school
    and ability of pupils 112
    Burnham unit total 27-30
    duties of teachers 183
    England and Wales, 176, 193
    in sample 21
    organization 39, 55, 56
    recommended minimum 25
    school councils 184
    sixth-form societies 184
    time spent on pupil welfare 58
Small schools
    ability grouping 66
    careers guidance 83
    contacts with community 172
    curriculum 78
    curriculum planning 45
    duties of teachers 183
    hours worked by staff 49, 58
    pupil welfare 36, 69
    school councils 184
    sixth-form societies 184
    staff allowances 32
Social class 17
    ability 98
    definitions 199
    extra-curricular activities 155
    4th year 76, 186
    in-group preference 123
    intake 69, 186
    popularity 120
Social evenings 169, 170
Social service 171
Sociometric study
    *see* friendship
Spanish 80, 82, 89, 92
Specialization 73, 97

Sport 171
    *see also* games, athletic events
Staff
    deployment 96, 94, 99
    employment 17, 25
    meetings 48
    qualifications 17
    ratios 26, 55
    turnover 26, 55
    welfare 48
Staying-on
    and staff salaries 34
Streams
    first-year ability 66
    fourth-year ability 74
    summary 98
    transfer between 17
Subject teaching 51
Supervision 49
Surveying 92
System
    traditional school organization 36
    house 37
    school and year 37
Teacher/pupil ratio
    *see* staff ratio
Teachers
    'classroom' 48-53, 183
    attendance at parents evenings 170
Technical drawing 73, 80, 89
Technical subjects 73
Theatre 169, 172
Theorists (educational) 18
Timetabling devices 61
Traditional system 36, 55
Transfer of pupils
    between forms 48
    between junior and senior high school 171
Tutors 70
Two-tier system 76
Typing 79, 80, 82
University entrance 84
Unstreaming 64, 69
Upper school 37
    *see* head of upper school
Urban schools 31, 53, 58, 63, 79, 83, 88, 110, 157, 172, 181, 183, 184
Use of English 96
Vernon Graded Arithmetic/Mathematics Test 101
Visitors to school 45

207

Visits
    industrial 84
    educational and cultural 172, 190, 191
    vocational 172, 190, 191
Voluntary extra-curricular activities
    *see* extra-curricular activities
Voluntary social work 173
    *see also* social service
Wales 52
    *see also* Welsh schools
Watts-Vernon English Reading Test 100
Welfare
    *see* Pupil Welfare
    staff 48
Welsh Reading Test 7, 101
Welsh schools 78
    age ranges 192
    careers prospects 83
    community contacts 170, 172, 189
    curriculum 78
    school councils 184

sixth form 88-90
sixth-form societies 184
staff-pupil ratio 181
versions of NF68 101
Woodwork 73, 79, 80, 89, 91, 92
'X' pupils
    attainment survey 105
    definition 26
    estimated percentages in intake 103, 187
    heads' estimates 103
    proportions in comprehensive schools 117
    staff allowances 32
    staff turnover 26
    time scheduled for lessons 53
Year systems 37, 56
Year teachers 38
    duties 182
    and pupil welfare 70
    staff allowances 31
Zoology 35, 89
'Z' pupils 105, 106, 117, 187